■ DRUGS
The Straight Facts

Hallucinogens

DRUGS The Straight Facts

Alcohol

Cocaine

Hallucinogens

Heroin

Marijuana

Nicotine

DRUGS
The Straight Facts

Hallucinogens

22407

Randi Mehling

Consulting Editor
David J. Triggle

University Professor
School of Pharmacy and Pharmaceutical Sciences
State University of New York at Buffalo

CHELSEA HOUSE
PUBLISHERS
A Haights Cross Communications Company
Philadelphia

CHELSEA HOUSE PUBLISHERS
VP, NEW PRODUCT DEVELOPMENT Sally Cheney
DIRECTOR OF PRODUCTION Kim Shinners
CREATIVE MANAGER Takeshi Takahashi
MANUFACTURING MANAGER Diann Grasse

Staff for HALLUCINOGENS
ASSOCIATE EDITOR Bill Conn
PRODUCTION EDITOR Jaimie Winkler
PHOTO EDITOR Sarah Bloom
SERIES & COVER DESIGNER Terry Mallon
LAYOUT 21st Century Publishing and Communications, Inc.

A Haights Cross Communications ◄ Company

http://www.chelseahouse.com

First Printing

1 3 5 7 9 8 6 4 2

Library of Congress Cataloging-in-Publication Data

Mehling, Randi.
  Hallucinogens / Randi Mehling.
    p. cm.
Includes index.
  ISBN 0-7910-7261-4
  1. Hallucinogenic drugs—Juvenile literature. I. Title.
RM324.8 .M447 2003
615'.7883—dc21

                                        2002153504

Table of Contents

The Use and Abuse of Drugs

The issues associated with drug use and abuse in contemporary society are vexing subjects, fraught with political agendas and ideals that often obscure essential information that teens need to know to have intelligent discussions about how to best deal with the problems associated with drug use and abuse. *Drugs: The Straight Facts* aims to provide this essential information through straightforward explanations of how an individual drug or group of drugs works in both therapeutic and non-therapeutic conditions; with historical information about the use and abuse of specific drugs; with discussion of drug policies in the United States; and with an ample list of further reading.

From the start, the series uses the word *"drug"* to describe psychoactive substances that are used for medicinal or non-medicinal purposes. Included in this broad category are substances that are legal or illegal. It is worth noting that humans have used many of these substances for hundreds, if not thousands of years. For example, traces of marijuana and cocaine have been found in Egyptian mummies; the use of peyote and Amanita fungi has long been a component of religious ceremonies worldwide; and alcohol production and consumption have been an integral part of many human cultures' social and religious ceremonies. One can speculate about why early human societies chose to use such drugs. Perhaps, anything that could provide relief from the harshness of life—anything that could make the poor conditions and fatigue associated with hard work easier to bear—was considered a welcome tonic. Life was likely to be, according to the seventeenth century English philosopher Thomas Hobbes, *"poor, nasty, brutish and short."* One can also speculate about modern human societies' continued use and abuse of drugs. Whatever the reasons, the consequences of sustained drug use are not insignificant—addiction, overdose, incarceration, and drug wars—and must be dealt with by an informed citizenry.

The problem that faces our society today is how to break

the connection between our demand for drugs and the willingness of largely outside countries to supply this highly profitable trade. This is the same problem we have faced since narcotics and cocaine were outlawed by the Harrison Narcotic Act of 1914, and we have yet to defeat it despite current expenditures of approximately $20 billion per year on "the war on drugs." The first step in meeting any challenge is always an intelligent and informed citizenry. The purpose of this series is to educate our readers so that they can make informed decisions about issues related to drugs and drug abuse.

SUGGESTED ADDITIONAL READING

David T. Courtwright, *Forces of Habit. Drugs and the making of the modern world.* Cambridge, Mass.: Harvard University Press, 2001. David Courtwright is Professor of History at the University of North Florida.

Richard Davenport-Hines, *The Pursuit of Oblivion. A global history of narcotics.* New York: Norton, 2002. The author is a professional historian and a member of the Royal Historical Society.

Aldous Huxley, *Brave New World.* New York: Harper & Row, 1932. Huxley's book, written in 1932, paints a picture of a cloned society devoted to the pursuit only of happiness.

David J. Triggle
University Professor
School of Pharmacy and Pharmaceutical Sciences
State University of New York at Buffalo

1

The History of Hallucinogens

Hundreds of species of plants contain the chemical substances we call hallucinogens, and have been altering the thoughts, moods, and perceptions of animals and people all over the world for thousands of years. A hallucinogen user may "see" a song, "hear" purple, or hold seemingly coherent conversations with family pets or house plants. A minute can feel like hours, and hours can feel like seconds. A user might become intrigued by a piece of furniture that appears to walk about the dining room, a wall that seems to breathe, or a rainbow of colors that appears streaming from his or her outstretched hand.

The ability to see visions, become more creative, discover deep insights, or witness "shadow" selves—the part of our inner selves that holds our darkest secrets—are often motivations to use hallucinogens. Some users report strong feelings of love and "connectedness" with all people, nature, and the planet, while others report feelings of depression, despair, and anxiety. Whether specifically used for healing and self-revelation, in religious ceremonies, or for pure pleasure and entertainment, hallucinogens create a mind-altering experience that advocates seek out while others swear "never again."

We do not have to dig too deeply to discover references to the use of hallucinogens throughout history. Researchers say ancient mushroom paintings found in the Sahara Desert may represent the first documented ritual use of hallucinogenic mushrooms by

Many cultures throughout history have used hallucinogens like these flowers from the morning glory plant, ipomoea violacea, in religious ceremonies and rituals. The Aztecs made a paste, called *teotlaqualli*, from the morning glory plant, which was rubbed on the skin of priests and soldiers. The Aztecs believed *teotlaqualli* helped priests and soldiers achieve the mental state necessary to serve their gods.

Paleolithic people 7,000 to 9,000 years ago. Giant mushroom statues have been found in Guatemala and El Salvador, dating back to 1000 B.C. Presumably, these statues were erected to pay homage to the spiritual powers of the psychedelic mushroom. The remains of hallucinogenic snuff and paraphernalia from 320 to 910 A.D. were discovered at an archeological site in Chile.

Many cultures have used hallucinogens to achieve mystical and spiritual wisdom. The Aztecs in pre-Columbian Mexico made a paste called *teotlaqualli* from the hallucinogenic flower *ololiuqui* (a part of the morning glory plant). Rubbed on the skin of Aztec priests and soldiers, ololiuqui was thought to eliminate fear and place the user in a proper mental state to serve the Aztec gods. Throughout the ages, peyote, a cactus whose above ground "button" portion contains a hallucinatory alkaloid, has been used ceremonially by the peoples of Mexico and, more recently, the Native Americans of the United States to attain closer spiritual communion.

Two thousand years ago, the ancient Athenians conducted secret nocturnal ceremonies in the temple at Eleusis to worship the goddesses Demeter and Persephone. Since initiates were sworn to secrecy, little is known of the rituals except that a drink called *kykeon*, a mixture of barley with water, mint, and ergot (from which LSD is derived), was noted as the focus of this annual event. Homer, author of the epic poems the *Iliad* and the *Odyssey*, described the ceremony as "a blissful experience that could lift men out of a gloomy darkness."

In many cultures, witch doctors or shamans have relied on "magical" plants to cure ailments and relieve pain that did not respond to more conventional treatments. Today, research is being conducted on the effects of MDMA (Ecstasy) in the treatment of post-traumatic stress disorder, and the active chemicals in psilocybin ("magic mushrooms") are being used in the treatment of cancer and other diseases.

Whether synthesized (man-made in a laboratory), or found naturally in plants, a hallucinogen is literally "a producer of hallucinations." It is no surprise, therefore, that the word *hallucinate* comes from the Latin verb *alucinari*, meaning "to wander in mind or attention" or "to dream," since the user's mind wanders from image to image as a result of the steady stream of sensory effects from hallucinogens.

In the 1950s, the term "psychotomimetic" was often used to describe the effects of hallucinogens. This was based on the belief that these substances made people temporarily insane, a belief that has subsequently been discredited. In fact, from the 1940s to the 1980s, hallucinogens were widely prescribed and used in the field of psychiatry to treat a variety of mental illnesses.

The term *psychedelic* was coined in the 1960s by British psychiatrist Humphry Osmond, who was studying the emotional effects of LSD and mescaline. The word originates from the Greek roots *psyche* (mind, soul) and *delos* (clear or visible) and is commonly interpreted to mean "mind revealing." The desire to search deeply into the mind and soul in order to understand the "self" with true clarity is a frequently reported motivation for using hallucinogens. Thus, we can see the connection between the spiritual and religious practices of ancient peoples and their use of hallucinogens, and more modern desires to "see within." Today, the terms *psychedelic* and *hallucinogen* are used interchangeably.

The myriad of hallucinogenic plants available in nature share a colorful history. More recently, laboratories have added to the plethora of hallucinogens available for human consumption by mimicking the hallucinogenic ingredients of these natural plants. In the following pages, we shall focus upon the history of some of the more well-known hallucinogens, both natural and synthetic, that are likely to be encountered by teenagers: LSD, psilocybin and psilocin, peyote and mescaline, and MDMA. The fly agaric mushroom

and PCP also are relevant to the human history of hallucinogens but will only be covered briefly in this historical
overview section.

LSD (LYSERGIC ACID DIETHYLAMIDE)

LSD is a drug manufactured from the principal active ingredi-
ent of ergot. Ergot is a parasitic fungus that infects rye, wheat,
and other grasses. This fungus itself is toxic—in fact, eating rye

HALLUCINOGENIC SLANG

Acid Head: LSD user

Babysit: Guide someone through a first drug experience

Come Home: End a trip on LSD

Graduate: To completely stop using drugs

Lit Up, Coasting, Flying, Hopped Up, Tripping:
Under the influence of drugs

LSD: Acid, Blotter, Lucy in the Sky with Diamonds,
Bart Simpsons, Contact Lens

MDMA: Ecstasy, X, Adam, XTC, Clarity, M&M, Love or
Hug Drug

Psilocybin, Psilocin: Magic Mushrooms, 'Shrooms,
Divine Flesh, Hombrecitos

Peyote, Mescaline: Mesc, Buttons, Cactus Head,
Half Moon, Shaman

Rave: A party designed to enhance a hallucinogenic
experience through music and dance

Totally Spent: MDMA hangover

X-ing: Using MDMA

Yen Sleep: Restless, drowsy state after LSD use

bread contaminated by ergot caused an epidemic that killed thousands of people in the Middle Ages.

In the 1930s, scientists at Sandoz Pharmaceutical Company in Switzerland were developing medicines derived from ergot and discovered compounds that were useful in treating migraine headaches as well as in obstetrics. For instance, certain ergot compounds were found to hasten childbirth by increasing uterine contractions. These medicines, however, did not have hallucinogenic qualities.

In 1938, the Swiss chemist Dr. Albert Hofmann, working for Sandoz, synthesized LSD-25, so named because it was the twenty-fifth compound made in this series of ergot derivatives. However, LSD's potent psychoactive properties were not discovered until five years later when, in 1943, Dr. Hofmann accidentally ingested a minute portion of the compound. Within about 40 minutes, he experienced the first reported LSD "trip," (a phrase coined from the "journey" that many users describe after ingesting a hallucinogen).

In 1949, Sandoz began marketing LSD-25 to psychiatrists in the United States for use in psychotherapy to help patients more quickly access repressed emotions. In the early 1950s, the U.S. Central Intelligence Agency (CIA) conducted human experiments with LSD (and several other types of hallucinogens) to determine its usefulness as an interrogation tool and a mind-control agent. (It was later discovered that a number of these CIA studies were conducted without the knowledge or consent of the participants.)

LSD use increased in the late 1950s and early 1960s, popularized by media and such "psychedelic gurus" as Timothy Leary, the former Harvard professor who was a vociferous proponent of LSD. Around 1965, citing public health concerns, the U.S. government banned LSD. Nonetheless, illegal manufacture and use of LSD continues today, and some research organizations are petitioning to re-open the study of LSD in the treatment of certain mental illnesses. LSD has also been reported to ease the fear and alienation experienced by dying patients; investigation is currently ongoing in this area.

PSILOCYBIN AND PSILOCIN (PSYCHEDELIC MUSHROOMS)

Psilocybin and psilocin are the hallucinogenic components of certain species of mushrooms found all over the world, especially in North, Central, and South America. Early users were so impressed by the effects of these mushrooms that they believed the fungi had divine origins. The sacred mushrooms of Mexico were called the *teonanactl*, or "flesh of the gods," by the Aztecs. Today, Mexican ceremonies combine shamanism and Roman Catholic ritual during nighttime, candlelight ceremonies. The shamans, usually women, conduct these services to treat illnesses, solve problems, and contact the "spirit" world.

PEYOTE AND MESCALINE

The peyote cactus became an integral part of sacred rituals for the Indians of Mexico before recorded history. The Aztecs of pre-Columbian Mexico used peyote "buttons" (the tops of the cactus, which are hallucinogenic) in religious rituals and as an antispasmodic. Use of the peyote cactus in health and spiritual practices spread to Native American groups in the United States during the nineteenth century. For example, the Mescalero Apaches of the southwestern United States practiced a peyote rite that was adopted by many of the Plains tribes.

In 1918, Native Americans organized what was formerly known as a "peyote cult" into a legally recognized religious group called the Native American Church of North America. Native American Church services usually begin after dark in *tipis* (teepees), take place around a fire, and last all night. These meetings include singing, chanting, and praying, as well as elements of Christian religious rituals. Peyote is eaten throughout the night, and participants pray to the spirit of the cactus.

This Native American man holds a peyote button—the top of a peyote cactus—which is hallucinogenic. Members of the Native American Church of North America believe that eating peyote in their religious practices gives them a greater awareness of God.

The Church's participants believe that eating the peyote will gain them a closer communion with God. In 1922, the Native American Church had 13,000 members; today, there are over 250,000 members in the United States and Canada. Native Americans who live far from peyote's natural habitat (the southwestern United States and northern Mexico) legally buy peyote buttons (also known as mescal buttons) that are distributed through the U.S. Postal Service. Since 1965, the U.S. government has given the Native American Church of North America legal permission to use peyote during religious ceremonies. (The right of members of the Native American Church to use peyote in their religious ceremonies has been challenged recently in federal court; however, its use still remains legal in certain states.)

Mescaline was isolated as one of the primary psychoactive components of peyote in 1896 by chemist Arthur Heffter. Aldous Huxley, author of *Brave New World* was among the first to extol the use of mescaline in controlled, medical settings. Huxley often experimented with the drug and wrote about his many mescaline experiences in such books as *The Doors of Perception*.

MDMA (METHYLENEDIOXY-METHAMPHETAMINE, ECSTASY)

A "designer drug," MDMA was created early in the twentieth century and patented by the pharmaceutical company Merck as a potential appetite suppressant. Though never brought to market, in the 1970s psychiatrists began using MDMA on patients after discovering its ability to assist the emotional healing process. According to one estimate, from the 1970s to the mid-1980s about 30,000 doses of MDMA were administered per month. Although illegal in the United States since 1985, MDMA—which has come to be known more commonly as Ecstasy—continues to be illicitly manufactured and distributed to those seeking euphoria and personal/spiritual growth. Under its influence, Ecstasy users may dance for hours at "rave" parties while feeling quite tender and loving toward themselves and everyone else, earning the drug's reputation as a "hug drug."

Although MDMA is not technically a hallucinogen, it is considered a "psychedelic amphetamine" and is currently one of the "drugs of choice" among teenage drug users; therefore, a significant portion of this book focuses on Ecstasy.

FLY AGARIC MUSHROOM (*AMANITA MUSCARIA*)

Since prehistoric times, ancient peoples have used the red-capped, white-spotted hallucinogenic mushroom called fly agaric (so named because a substance in the mushroom kills flies) as part of shamanistic rituals. Shamans were priests who acted as a the link to the spirit world. After drinking the extract from this mushroom, shamans translated the divine will and prophecies of the gods for their fellow tribesmen. Since this mushroom is native to Siberia, some say the word *shaman* originated there with these rites. It is hypothesized that Siberian nomads brought shamanism to the Americas when they journeyed across the Bering Strait about 15,000 years ago.

Other interesting history tells us that Norse Vikings ate fly agaric before going into battle to produce "ecstatic reckless rage" for which they earned the nickname *berserkers.* Reindeer of that region still fight each other over the chance to eat these mycologic mysteries. This psychedelic mushroom is so potent that the urine of those animals, which is ingested by humans, is just as hallucinogenic as the mushroom itself. Therefore, the drug could be, and was, recycled among tribal members.

This importance of the fly agaric mushroom extends throughout the world. The Hindu holy book, *Rig Veda*, mentions *soma*, a sacred substance used to induce higher levels of consciousness. Soma is thought to have been derived

The red-capped, white-spotted mushroom known as fly agaric has been consumed throughout the ages for its hallucinogenic effects. Shamans from Siberia used these mushrooms as a link to the spiritual world, Vikings ate fly agaric mushrooms before going into battle, and Hindu scriptures make reference to its use to achieve higher levels of consciousness.

from the juice of the fly agaric mushroom, and it is believed to have been brought to the ancient tribes of India about 3,500 years ago by Aryan invaders who worshipped the hallucinogen and drank its extract during sacred rites.

PCP (PHENCYCLIDINE)

Although PCP is often classified as a hallucinogen, it rarely produces LSD-like hallucinations; in fact, it belongs to a unique class of drugs called "dissociative anesthetics." Originally developed in the 1950s as a potent horse tranquilizer, PCP was later tested on human subjects as an anesthetic. Eventually, it was abandoned because of its "severe and unpredictable" side effects, including psychotic and violent behavior. Since PCP is not technically a hallucinogen and is not widely used by teenage drug users, it will not be the subject of further discussion in this book.

2

The Psychedelic Effects of Hallucinogens

WHAT ARE HALLUCINOGENS?

We interpret the world through our senses, by seeing, smelling, touching, hearing, and tasting. Despite a diverse cultural history, hallucinogens have one property in common: they distort or alter the way we perceive the world through our senses. These distortions are commonly referred to as hallucinations and can affect not only our sensory perceptions, but our thoughts and feelings as well.

(As a reminder, when speaking about hallucinogens, we will be specifically referring to LSD, psilocybin and psilobin, peyote and mescaline, and MDMA.)

According to its exact definition, a hallucination occurs when a person hears or sees something that does not exist but *believes* that this distortion of reality is, in fact, reality. This inability to distinguish reality as perceived by others is known typically as a psychosis. A variety of situations such as great fatigue or severe emotional stress, and even disease states such as schizophrenia or running a high fever, can cause hallucinations.

Many experts believe that the term hallucinogen is a misnomer, arguing that a hallucinogen causes neither hallucinations nor psychoses. (Remember that in the 1950s, this class of drugs was

In the movie *A Beautiful Mind*, actor Russell Crowe portrayed John Nash, a brilliant mathematician who experienced psychotic hallucinations that he thought were real. A hallucinogenic drug user, however, is usually able to recognize that his or her drug-induced hallucinations are not real.

referred to as psychotomimetics—substances that mimic psychosis.) The major distinction between "true" and drug-inspired hallucinations is that the hallucinogen user usually remains *aware* that the hallucination is actually an illusion created by the drug and is not really representative of the normal everyday world. If the user loses that grip on reality and believes that the altered sensations are real and not illusory, he or she can "freak out" and have a panic or anxiety attack. For example, LSD typically distorts visual imagery. An LSD user might see a friend's face melt or a Dali-esque clock with dripping numbers, but usually understands that it is the drug that is producing these "perceptions."

There has been great debate over what to call the class of drugs that produces hallucinogenic "illusions." For the purposes of this text, we will define hallucinogens as a group of drugs whose principal effects are the production of altered or distorted mental states and refer to them as either hallucinogens or psychedelics.

PSYCHOLOGICAL EFFECTS OF PSYCHEDELICS

Hallucinogens do not necessarily produce any particular mood or frame of mind. Instead, they tend to intensify a user's experiences. If taken when happy, hallucinogens tend to make the user feel incredibly happy. If taken when depressed, a user may experience feelings of "super-depression." Hallucinogens can also unbearably intensify feelings of distrust or dislike as well.

The effects of hallucinogens on the human psyche are well documented. Personal accounts of "tripping on acid" have been recorded in our modern times since Dr. Hofmann himself experimented with LSD and described his experiences to his colleagues. It is logical to expect the psychological effects of these mind-altering substances to be quite subjective and personal, as varied, in fact, as the millions of individuals who have taken these drugs.

Although the psychedelic of hallucinogens are diverse, there are many shared experiences among users. These psychological effects have been grouped into categories by researchers who are interested in understanding the mental effects of hallucinogens.

Eidetic Imagery

Eidetic images have been described as "eyeball movies" or "your own private movie theater" since the hallucinogen user "sees" physical objects while his or her eyes are closed. These images may appear as abstract designs, such as a pattern in a rug that keeps repeating endlessly, making it appear as if the whole rug is moving. The hallucinogen user might feel nervous about walking across this moving set of rug patterns, and fail to understand how someone else, who is not under the drug's influence, can walk over the carpet with ease. Eidetic images often appear repeatedly, giving the hallucinogen user a seemingly "endless" film loop that plays over and over again in his or her mind.

Synesthesia

The hallucinogen user may experience synesthesia—an altered perception of the world that blends normally distinct senses. Most frequently, a user translates sounds to mean colors; for example, as someone claps their hands, the user might see flashes of color timed to the meeting of the hands.

Depersonalization

Hallucinogen users often feel detached from their bodies and report having "out of body experiences." This often includes a feeling that one's body is not one's own, or that the user's body is really next to him or her or even levitating. This perception can interfere with physical coordination.

Separation from Self

Some hallucinogen users report feeling the boundaries between themselves and their environment disappear, leading to a sense of oneness or wholeness with the universe, a type of "cosmic consciousness." This experience is also reported as a "transcendence of the self," where space, time, and identity are perceived as "rearranged." This is often interpreted as a mystical, religious, or metaphysical experience, yielding profound personal insights.

Simultaneous Extreme Sensations

The emotional and physical world is experienced much more extremely while under the influence of hallucinogens. Users can experience both "good" and "bad" sensations while tripping, often at the same time. Sensations of every conceivable sort can bombard the user; for instance, one can be thrust from horror, to rapture, to fear, to empowerment—seemingly at the same moment in time. These effects can be very unsettling to some users. What is felt as pleasant becomes a "magic voyage to the gods;" what is normally felt as unpleasant becomes a "trip to the fiery depths of hell." Perhaps this is why mescaline user Aldous Huxley named a book of his experiences *Heaven and Hell*.

Multi-level Reality

Sometimes a person who has taken a hallucinogen perceives an object on a number of different levels simultaneously. One hallucinogen user, for example, reported that while sitting on a chair he could see "right through things to the molecules." For many hallucinogen users, these drugs allow thoughts to be processed on many levels at the same time, facilitating deep introspection, spiritual communion, and problem-solving. However, some users report that this "speeding up" of analysis and thought processing can lead to highly unpleasant experiences such as confusion, disorientation, fear, and panic. The unpredictable nature of "good and bad" trips while on hallucinogens is a subject we will turn to later in this chapter.

Aldous Huxley, the author of *Brave New World* and *Doors of Perception*, experimented with mescaline and wrote about his hallucinogenic experiences in *Heaven and Hell*, a book whose title suggests that Huxley understood the extreme emotions that the hallucinogenic drug user may experience.

Subjective Exaggeration

Objects, events, moods, people, situations—many experiences, in fact—are often perceived in an exaggerated form when using hallucinogens. This exaggeration may be in sheer number—for example, one flower might "bloom" into 50 flowers instantly. Or, an imaginative mind could turn a towel falling off the bed into a lizard crawling down the bedspread. Users have also cited "eureka" experiences in which ordinary objects or events are experienced as profound and extraordinary, thus intensifying the experience.

Emotional Lability

Many psychedelic users experience great mood swings, known as emotional lability. Under the drug's influence, a person can suddenly shift from ecstasy to crushing depression. Within seconds, laughing can become sobbing and then swing back to happiness a few seconds later.

Timelessness

Many hallucinogen users report a sense of timelessness. They feel that time ceases to exist or suddenly feels irrelevant. Concepts such as hours, minutes, clocks, and schedules become incomprehensible and meaningless.

Irrationalism

Intuition, emotional communication, touch, empathy, and subjectivity can take on a "cosmic" and profound significance for hallucinogenic users when compared to the more "rational" concepts of logic, cause-and-effect relationships, and objectivity. Many users report a greater connection not only with fellow humans, but with all members of the planet: animal, plant, or mineral. Communicating via words can become meaningless and even offensively harsh.

"Virtual" Hallucinations

While hallucinogens induce what are described as hallucinations, these are not hallucinations (as we have discussed) in the strictest sense. Hence, some researchers add the word "virtual" when explaining the effect of hallucinogenic drugs on the user. A typical example of a "virtual" hallucination is the frequently reported altered perception of the user's own body (and of other people's bodies as well) into various, unusual and "never-before-seen" states. Users report experiences such as looking into a mirror and watching their face morph from a 16-year-old's to an 80-year-old's or seeing a man with a frog's head walking down the street.

Sensory Overload

Normally, our brains allow us to filter and limit what we perceive so that we may choose to focus upon a particular set of sensations from the world around us. LSD, for example, interferes with the functioning of a structure in the brain called the *reticular formation* which provides this sensory filter. After taking hallucinogens, many sensations are no longer filtered, and the mind is flooded with images, sounds, feelings and other sensory input that the user might normally not pay attention to. This strongly influences the user's ability to "think straight."

Flashbacks

When a person has a flashback, he or she experiences a psychedelic effect in the absence of taking a hallucinogen. While most people who have used hallucinogens never experience a flashback, a few do. Flashbacks reportedly appear suddenly and last for a few seconds or minutes and are typically visual illusions, such as trails of light, or as distorted time sequences. Extreme fatigue, emotional stress, or the use of such drugs as marijuana or alcohol can also provoke flashbacks.

SET AND SETTING

Because of the highly subjective nature of the hallucinogenic experience, the psychedelic effects of hallucinogens are

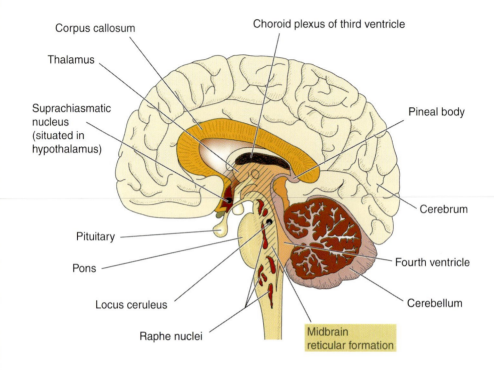

Corpus callosum

Thalamus

Suprachiasmatic
nucleus
(situated in
hypothalamus)

Choroid plexus of third ventricle

Pineal body

Cerebrum

Pituitary

Pons

Locus ceruleus

Raphe nuclei

Fourth ventricle

Cerebellum

Midbrain
reticular formation

LSD interferes with the reticular formation, a section of the midbrain
that acts as a sensory filter. When the reticular formation malfunctions,
sensations can appear distorted and jumbled. This causes the user to
experience vivid hallucinations, such as colors that accompany sounds,
furniture that moves or melts, or other altered perceptions. These perceptions can occur within 20 minutes after taking a dose of LSD, and
last 6-8 hours. Some users experience hallucinations that are so frightening and disturbing that they are reluctant to try the drug again.

extremely dependent upon the user's expectations about
using the drug (the "set") and the physical, social, and
cultural surroundings in which the drug is being taken
(the setting).

Set

Set is a person's expectation for the type of effect he or she will experience after using a hallucinogen. This expectation is created by a person's total past experience—all that he or she has ever heard, read, seen, or thought about in reference to encounters with hallucinogens. Sometimes teenagers (just like adults) do not really know what their true feelings are about using hallucinogens. One could feel eager to "fit in" with friends and think using Ecstasy or LSD is cool, but deep down be really scared of what might happen—of losing control, for example. Based on the conscious and unconscious expectations brought to a given situation, a person's underlying feelings can strongly influence the effect of a hallucinogenic experience.

Setting

Setting is a person's physical, social, and cultural environment. For thousands of years, the hallucinogenic plants of North and South America have been used in socially accepted ways for medicinal, religious, and psychoactive purposes. In these cultures, each member of the community is taught from an early age the purpose of taking hallucinogens and what to expect afterwards. This cultural and social expectation is also an important aspect of set and can define a hallucinogenic experience as positive or negative.

A user's expectations and cultural surroundings are relevant to understanding the psychedelic experience in another way; it seems to take practice to know how to "be high." Each individual needs to understand and define what the expectations are for "being high" since the effects of drugs are specific to people, places, and times. In other words, people have to "learn" to associate changes of consciousness with drug use in order to "know" that is indeed what they are experiencing.

DOSE

Dose is another critical component in understanding the psychological and physical effects of hallucinogens, since all effects are highly dose-dependent. To understand the role of dose, it is important to note that any substance—from drugs to water—can benefit or harm a person, depending upon its quantity, quality, and potency. High doses of a substance can produce very different effects from low doses. Water is necessary for human life; but drink extreme amounts of water in a short period of time and the electrolyte and other critical balances in the body may be disrupted with negative consequences.

Also, size does matter; a person who weighs 100 pounds may experience deleterious or even fatal effects from a drug while someone who weighs 165 pounds may take the same dose of the drug without adverse effect. Many medicines are beneficial at low doses but deadly at high doses. In fact, low doses of LSD, MDMA, and other hallucinogens were regularly prescribed from the 1950s to the 1980s to treat a variety of mental health disorders.

Researchers now know that some hallucinogens may not cause the user to experience characteristic "hallucinations" at very low doses; instead, users experience a "gentler" psychedelic trip. Higher doses, however, do magnify all effects of all hallucinogens and, therefore, are more frequently related to the occurrences of a bad trip.

PHYSICAL EFFECTS

Although the psychological effects of hallucinogens are often quite subjective, their physical effects are more constant, primarily because psychedelics have similar ways of chemically interacting within our bodies. Typically, hallucinogens can cause feelings of "butterflies" in the stomach, nausea, vomiting, cold hands and feet, numbness in the face and lips, and changes in coordination. Increased alertness and wakefulness are also characteristic stimulant effects of many hallucinogens, as are pupil dilation, jitteriness, and a suppression of appetite (more aptly described as a lack of interest in food). These drugs also raise blood pressure, heart rate, and body temperature (which is especially the case with MDMA). Many of the naturally occurring hallucinogens found in mushrooms and peyote are bitter and commonly cause nausea and vomiting.

It is important to note that while hallucinogens share very similar physical effects, the degree to which each physical effect is experienced varies greatly from one psychedelic to another. This is because the duration of each hallucinogenic "high" varies. Users of LSD often report extreme fatigue the day after tripping and require long periods of rest and sleep. Researchers believe this feeling of exhausion is the result of the 12-hour trip that LSD users experience. Because of its shorter duration of psychedelic action (four to six hours), MDMA does not produce the same day-after fatigue. However, long-time MDMA users report an increased sensitivity to day-after fatigue as they get older, along with an increased susceptibility to colds and infections.

In addition to the effect of dose, the combination of alcohol (and/or other drugs) with hallucinogens increases the possibility of unpredictable and unpleasant physical effects of a hallucinogenic experience.

THE UNPREDICTABILITY OF HALLUCINOGENS

There is never any certainty, nor any real ability, to predict the effects of a hallucinogenic experience. Despite the expectations, dosage, and setting associated with the person and the drug-taking event, a user might take the same amount of LSD in the same setting with the same friends at the same time of the day and have a radically different experience compared with a previous drug-taking experience. The first event could have been "peaceful and rewarding," the second, "frightening and disturbing." Even frequent hallucinogen users report this unpredictability. One could take a hallucinogen 25 times with positive associations, yet on the twenty-sixth occasion have a negative experience.

In reality, it turns out that most trips contain both "good" and "bad" moments. Interestingly, it often takes only one profoundly bad trip for some teens to stop taking hallucinogens altogether. As a result of the unpredictable nature

CONVENTIONAL-UNCONVENTIONAL: Can Personality Predict Drug Use?

Researchers created a scale of "conventionality-unconventionality" in an attempt to categorize the personality differences between adolescent drug users and non-users. The basic personality traits of young adolescents were identified prior to their use of any drugs. Based on these personality traits, the adolescents were put into one of two groups: conventional and unconventional. In contrast to the conventional students, the unconventional students showed greater concern for personal independence, a lack of interest in the goals of institutions such as school or church, and a jaundiced view of the larger society around them. Predictions were then made on who would use drugs (unconventional personality) and who would not (conventional personality).

Several years later, the same adolescents were studied again, and the accuracy of the researchers proved extremely high. The unconventional personality emerged as a key factor in drug experimentation and use among the adolescents. The study indicated that drug use and unconventionality were directly linked: the more unconventional the youth, the greater the likelihood of drug experimentation. In addition, the study indicated that the more unconventional adolescents have a greater chance of developing a more serious drug involvement.

of the hallucinogenic trip, the fear of suffering another profoundly bad experience outweighed the desire of these teens to experience a potentially good trip.

Personality also greatly influences the outcome of a hallucinogenic experience, since each individual has his or her own tolerance for handling the different distortions and altered perceptions inherent in hallucinogenic effects. People who grow up in families with a strong hold on their emotions and tight definitions of what are "real" or "normal" experiences are more likely to feel anxiety when their "traditional moorings" are cut free during the hallucinogen experience. (This is a fine example of set!)

ACUTE AND CHRONIC EFFECTS: A DISCUSSION

Short-term, acute effects describe a condition that is temporary and short-lived; long-term, chronic effects are cumulative and can last a lifetime.

There are consequences to the short-term effects of hallucinogens that can greatly influence a teen's long-term future. Although the hallucinogenic high eventually ends, and therefore is considered temporary, in real-world settings such as the classroom, a hallucinogenic trip can have lasting consequences. The structured activities of the classroom demand clear perception, reasoning, and recall. A student who is not in full control of his or her faculties will likely fail to perform to the best of his or her abilities in a classroom situation. It is reasonable to assume that a student who consistently attends school while high will find it difficult to retain the valuable information needed for such future endeavors as college or a professional trade.

Additionally, it is important to be aware that hallucinogens can cause accidental injuries or death due to impaired or distorted perceptions, physical coordination, and decision-making abilities. Driving, operating heavy machinery, or being in a dangerous locale or with dangerous people can turn a supposedly good trip into a nightmare. Simply experiencing the extrasensory effects of hallucinogens, and believing, for example, that one can "fly," could lead to a hallucinogenic-related injury or possibly death.

Although many of the short-term psychological effects of hallucinogens (such as increased awareness of music, joy, and other sensory experiences) can seem fun and interesting to some, researchers stress that the acute effects of anxiety, panic attacks, feelings of paranoia, and confusion are equally likely outcomes of hallucinogen use and cannot be predicted.

Researchers point out that the chronic effects of heavy LSD use (use of the drug once a week for several years) often included sleep disturbances due to the stimulating and "wakeful" activity of the drug, loss of appetite and energy, and an "unraveling" of personal connections. The heavy user is portrayed by some researchers as detached from the normal world of his or her peers and losing control in many areas of life.

Most heavy LSD users remain unaware of this increasing disorganization of their lives. Signs of a chronic user can include an inability to deal with timeliness (which can negatively affect the user's ability to hold down a job or attend school successfully), as well as a lack of concern over personal appearance and hygiene. In fact, LSD often masks its long-term negative effects, leading the user to think it is the LSD that is creating an *illusion* of a life unraveling when in fact the drug is actually *causing* a very real downward spiral.

Research shows that many teen LSD users abandon the drug when this life disruption becomes so great that it can no longer be ignored. For example, one former teen user finally understood that she could not live in her "disconnected" teenage life forever, recognizing that she was failing in high school and needed to "grow up." In this case, we see that the loss of control was viewed by the teen user as no longer a "positive" aspect of the hallucinogenic experience. Rather, this loss of control was causing a disconnectedness that would likely lead to future problems and unhappiness in the teen user's life.

3

The Properties of Hallucinogens

HALLUCINOGENS AND THE HUMAN BODY

Pharmacologists investigate the effects of drugs on the human body, often using results from animal studies to predict drug reactions in humans. The dose of the drug, its route of exposure (ingestion versus inhalation, for example), the duration of the drug's effects, how the drug interacts with the different organ systems within the body, and other variables are studied to determine how a person will respond to a drug.

Certain hallucinogens share similar chemical structures and are often classified accordingly. For simplicity's sake, this book will classify these drugs in the same manner. Since mescaline and MDMA have a similar chemical configuration to amphetamines (stimulants), we will consider them as one group; LSD and psilocybin and psilocin fall into their own, separate category. The reader should be aware that there are many other hallucinogens that fall into these two categories; however, those drugs remain outside the scope of this book.

There are some interesting differences between the two groups of hallucinogens. For example, the psychedelic effects of LSD and hallucinogenic mushrooms occur rapidly, usually within 40 minutes of ingestion, whereas the onset of the effects from the amphetamine-related hallucinogens, MDMA, and mescaline, are more gradual. (As an interesting aside, mescaline is the only naturally occurring compound in the amphetamine-related hallucinogens group; all the rest, including MDMA, are synthesized in laboratories.)

LSD

(d-lysergic acid diethylamide)

This is the chemical structure of LSD, $C_{20}H_{25}N_{3}O$, a semi-synthetic drug not found in nature. It is derived from lysergic acid, a natural fungus that grows on rye, wheat, and similar grasses.

LSD (LYSERGIC ACID DIETHYLAMIDE)

LSD is a semi-synthetic drug not found in nature; it is produced in a laboratory. LSD is derived from lysergic acid, a chemical found in ergot (*Claviceps purpurea*), a natural fungus that grows on most rye, wheat, and similar grasses. Lysergic acid on its own is not hallucinogenic, however; in fact, it is used in several medicinal compounds.

Dose

LSD is one of the most potent drugs known. As little as ten micrograms can loosen inhibitions and create mild euphoria and empathetic feeling. (By way of comparison, an average postage stamp weighs about 60,000 micrograms.) Doses of 70–140 micrograms in a 155-pound person can produce LSD's characteristic perceptual and psychic effects. The drug's most intense psychic effect, the sense of contacting some profound "universal truth," occurs at higher doses. The dose common in the early 1960s (when achieving this "universal consciousness" was often a motivation for LSD use) was 250 micrograms, which is the same dose that Dr. Hofmann ingested during his experiments with LSD. In the 1990s, a dose of LSD averaged about 50 micrograms. Weight for weight, LSD is reported to be anywhere from 1,000 to 5,000 times as potent as mescaline, and 100 to 200 times as potent as psilocybin. (Potency refers to the strength of a drug's effects.)

Route of Exposure

Ingestion is the most common route into the body for any hallucinogen. LSD is ingested in a wide array of forms: small tablets of all colors ("microdots"); tiny squares of gelatin ("windowpanes"); and, most commonly, paper soaked in solutions of the drug and stamped with cartoonish ink designs ("blotter acid"). Liquid LSD is sometimes put onto a sugar cube, an aspirin, or a breath mint.

LSD is easily absorbed through the gastrointestinal tract, and the drug is quickly released to all tissues in the body, including the brain. Only about one percent of LSD's metabolites that are eliminated as urine still contain hallucinogenic properties.

Lethal Dose

Although there have been no documented overdose deaths related to LSD, pharmacologists have established a lethal dose

(LD) for the drug. Called the LD^{50}, this is the subscript dose at which half the test animals died after taking LSD. Applying this animal-based data to humans, scientists have established an LD^{50} of 14,000 micrograms of LSD in a 155-pound person. This means that a person of average weight would have to ingest 280 of the 50-microgram doses, more than 30 pounds, to overdose on LSD. Most experts agree, however, that it would be very difficult to ingest such a large volume of LSD at one time.

Duration of Effects

LSD's effects begin to be noticed about 30–40 minutes after ingestion; they peak two to five hours later and may continue for eight to twelve hours or more, often ebbing and returning several times. An increased dose will affect the duration and intensity of LSD's psychological and physical effects.

The duration of psychedelic effects *for all hallucinogens* is

THE PSYCHEDELIC SEEDS OF THE MORNING GLORY

The closest naturally occurring substance to LSD is called ergine, or lysergic acid amide, found in the seeds of certain varieties of the morning glory flower. The psychedelic effects from these seeds are much weaker than LSD, so it requires hundreds of the seeds to produce a noticeable mind-altering effect. Because the coating of these seeds is indigestible, the seeds must be cracked or ground up to release the drug, which is usually prepared as a tea. These seeds are also mildly toxic and frequently cause nausea, vomiting, and other unpleasant side effects. Although morning glory seeds are easily and legally available, many varieties have been treated with poisonous pesticides and other chemicals to discourage people from eating them.

dependent on the time it takes the liver to metabolize the drug so it can then be excreted through the feces, sweat, and urine. At the present time, there is no drug that can be given, nor any substance ingested, to halt a trip that has begun; thus, a user must see a trip through to its completion.

Half-lives are important in understanding the length of time a drug stays active in the body. The half-life of LSD—the time it takes half of the drug to metabolize and then be excreted from the body—is about five hours. Comparatively, heroin and cocaine are metabolized much more quickly; their half-lives are 30 and 50 minutes, respectively.

Manufacture

Skill, equipment, and access to lysergic acid are required to manufacture LSD illegally. A batch of 25 to 100 grams (0.5 to 2 million dosages, based on a standard dosage of 50 micrograms) can be made in two to three days. The average price is $3 to $6 for a dose.

Because LSD is a manufactured drug, there is no assurance that what is being sold as LSD is actually pure. "Bad acid," or LSD mixed with drugs or chemicals other than LSD, is cited as a significant cause of bad trips that lead to distressing or harmful physical and psychological effects. A bad trip can end up creating such a state of anxiety or severe physical reactions that the "trip" taken is to the nearest emergency room.

A pill, capsule, or powder purporting to be LSD might, in fact, combine any number of ingredients. Laboratory analyses of blood from people admitted to hospitals for LSD emergencies show that in some urban areas, only about 50 percent of the drug samples actually contained LSD. Strychnine, PCP, and amphetamine are common and potentially dangerous additives. Strychnine, for instance, has been used historically as rat poison and can cause seizures and convulsions. Depending on the dose of the drug ingested, these impurities can have serious consequences.

PSILOCYBIN AND PSILOCIN (PSYCHEDELIC MUSHROOMS)

Psychedelic mushrooms containing psilocybin and psilocin grow naturally in many parts of the world, including Europe, Southeast Asia, Central and South America, Mexico, along the Gulf Coast, and in much of the southeastern United States. More than a dozen species of hallucinogenic mushrooms grow in the fields and woods of the Pacific Northwest. In fact, researchers have identified over 90 mushroom species that contain psilocybin and psilocin, with more still being discovered. The most commonly ingested hallucinogenic mushroom species in the United States are *Psilocybe mexicana* and *Psilocybe cyanescens.*

Dose

Estimates vary, but a typical dose of psilocybin is four to ten milligrams (two to four of the *Psilocybe cyanescens* mushroom). Psychedelic mushrooms vary greatly in their potency. Because of this, it can be difficult to gauge a dose that will provide psychedelic effects within a desired comfort level. These effects are unpredictable and depend not only on the quantity of the mushroom consumed, but also upon the type, size, and age of the mushroom. One medium-sized mushroom of a potent strain may give the same effect as twenty of a mild strain. Psilocybin is about 30 times more potent than mescaline and only about one percent as potent as LSD.

Route of Exposure

Psilocybin is usually available as a mushroom and sometimes as a white powder. Hallucinogenic mushrooms are difficult to digest raw and are reported to have a horrible taste.

Although many people think that psilocybin is the active psychedelic component of these "magic mushrooms," this is a mistaken view. Once ingested, the psilocybin is

Psychedelic mushrooms grow naturally in many parts of the world and vary greatly in their potency. Factors such as the strain, type, size, and age of the mushroom, as well as the quantity of mushrooms consumed, have the potential to affect the user's hallucinogenic experience.

metabolized in the liver into psilocin; therefore, psilocin is actually the primary hallucinogenic component of psilocybin. This hallucinogenic metabolite eventually makes its way to the brain. Psilocin is 1.4 times as potent as psilocybin. A lethal overdose is unlikely since a fatal dose is equal to more than 2,000 times the psychoactive dose.

Duration of Effects

The physical effects of mushrooms are a milder, gentler version of those experienced with LSD. The hallucinogenic effects of mushrooms begin about 30 to 40 minutes after ingestion and peak in about two hours, with the experience lasting anywhere from two to six hours.

Manufacture

Pure psilocybin was manufactured by several Swiss pharmaceutical companies, but underground (illegal) manufacturers found it too costly to produce. In recent years, kits of the spores necessary to grow these hallucinogenic mushrooms have been widely sold through the mail and in stores; since the spores themselves do not contain psilocybin, they are not technically illegal.

It is important to be aware that it requires considerable education and skill to properly identify and differentiate the hundreds of different mushrooms growing in nature. Many mushroom species are poisonous and even lethal. Some species contain toxins that can cause liver and kidney failure. The testing kits that are sold to assist in learning whether a mushroom contains psilocybin are not dependable. Even mushrooms sold in "starter kits" have a potential for toxicity.

PEYOTE AND MESCALINE

Peyote (or *peyotl*) is one of the oldest psychedelic agents known and is the name for a small, spineless cactus with white, hairy tufts called *Lophophra williamsii* or *Anhalonium lewinii*. It is light blue-green, bears small pink flowers, and has a carrot-shaped root. Its natural habitat is in the desert environments of the southwestern United States and northern Mexico. The top of the cactus looks mushroom-like, and is cut off and dried into peyote "buttons" (also known as mescal buttons). These buttons retain their hallucinogenic potency for a long time.

Dose

The estimated dose of peyote is about six to twelve buttons, although some research puts the effective dose at 200 mg, or about three to five buttons. Mescaline is estimated to be anywhere from 1,000 to 5,000 times less potent than LSD.

Route of Exposure

Peyote buttons are typically ingested. Although the dried button of the cactus is the usual form of eating peyote, it is also ground into powders or made into tea. It can be smoked, but this is unusual. Peyote has a nauseating, bitter taste that makes most first time users vomit. The Native Americans who use peyote in their religious ceremonies typically fast before eating it for this reason. Some members of the Native American Church say that when used repeatedly over time during religious services, the nausea and vomiting from peyote eventually subside.

Researchers explain that the nauseating physical effects of peyote are a result of over 40 psychoactive components contained in the peyote cactus; out of these, mescaline is the primary psychoactive compound. To avoid or lessen this nauseous reaction, peyote is normally swallowed whole without chewing. There is a myth that the white stringy hairs inside the peyote buttons actually contain strychnine which is responsible for the nauseous effects of the drug. However, these hairs are really just plant fibers that are just not digestible, but are not poisonous.

Duration of Effects

Mescaline's effects—similar to those of LSD—appear within about an hour of ingestion and can last up to 12 hours.

Since mescaline has a chemical structure related to amphetamine, which is a stimulant, it is not surprising that mescaline shares many of amphetamine's stimulating physical effects as well, such as increased heart rate and blood pressure. However, the psychological hallucinogenic effects of mescaline are more similar to those experienced with LSD. It is interesting to note that, although the behavioral effects and duration of LSD and mescaline are similar, mescaline is considerably less potent than LSD.

Members of the Native American Church attend ceremonies that involve the use of peyote, like this ceremony held in a teepee in Mirando City, Texas. Church members often fast before eating peyote to combat the nausea and vomiting that accompany peyote consumption.

Manufacture

Mescaline can be manufactured in a laboratory. When it has been synthesized, it looks like "long, needle-like white crystals." In this manufactured form, mescaline can be eaten in a powder, tablet, capsule, or liquid form. Mescaline costs more than LSD on the street; as a result, many drug dealers will attempt to pass off LSD as mescaline to unsuspecting buyers.

MDMA (METHYLENEDIOXYMETHAMPHETAMINE)

Due to its increasingly widespread usage among teenagers, MDMA (Ecstasy) is viewed as one of the most pressing drug problems in the United States today. Labeled "the hug drug," this synthesized substance has also lead some researchers to categorize it as an "enactogen" for the increased feelings of empathy, openness, love, and "connectedness" it inspires in its users (who also report a decrease in fear, defensiveness, and aggression). It makes sense, then, that the word enactogen is derived from the Latin roots *en* (within), *gen* (to produce), and *tactus* (touch).

Scientists who were originally studying mescaline in the laboratory created MDMA, along with many similar drugs called "analogs." Structurally related to mescaline, MDMA is an amphetamine-based hallucinogen that can produce both stimulant and hallucinogenic effects.

Dose

Estimates of MDMA doses in pill form vary from 50 mg up to 200 to 300 mg, although many researchers have called 125 mg an average dose. Low doses are associated with the more classic enactogen effects of tenderness and openness. Higher doses move the user into the more classic LSD-like hallucinogenic effects and increase MDMA's stimulating amphetamine effects as well. It is difficult to know with assurance the exact dose of MDMA in each pill, increasing the likelihood that a user may unknowingly take a larger dose than is either expected or can be handled.

Route of Exposure

Users of MDMA ingest pills that are often available in different colors, although on rare occasions pure powder is dissolved in water and injected. After it is digested, MDMA is absorbed from the gastrointestinal tract.

Duration of Effects

The hallmark effects of MDMA usually arrive about 30 minutes to an hour after it is ingested; its effects last for three to six hours. It requires almost two days (about 40 hours) for over 95 percent of MDMA to be cleared from the body.

Manufacture

Illegal drug laboratories alter the structure of amphetamine to "design" MDMA and several other related drugs. Since the drug is synthesized, its purity and potency can vary from one location to another. These clandestine laboratories often manufacture pills that look exactly like Ecstasy but actually combine small amounts of MDMA with other drugs such as PMA, MDA (a "sister" drug to MDMA), amphetamines, or caffeine. PMA (paramethoxyamphetamine) is an illegal amphetamine derivative that has similar but weaker effects than MDMA. As a result, users looking to increase the psychedelic effects of what they think is MDMA may take a second pill; unfortunately, PMA escalates body temperature dramatically and has been implicated in a number of deaths.

There are kits available to test an MDMA pill for authenticity. The kit contains a chemical called "Marquis reagent." A small solution is prepared by adding a drop of this chemical to a scraping of an Ecstasy pill. The solution will turn a particular color if certain drugs are present. These kits reveal whether a pill contains any Ecstasy-like substances or if the pill is completely fake; however, these tests do not show how much Ecstasy is actually in the pill.

Purity, Dose, and Physical Effects: A Special Note on MDMA

Commonly taken at raves (all-night parties), the stimulating, amphetamine-like nature of MDMA increases the user's energy, stamina, and wakefulness, greatly enhancing the ability to dance for long periods of time without tiring. This increased physical exertion can dramatically increase the already inherent physical effects of the drug—elevated blood pressure, heart rate, and body temperature. In combination with traditionally cramped and poorly ventilated club venues, the MDMA user's body temperature can elevate to dangerous levels, leading to possible organ failure, seizures, or even death. Additive chemicals (such as PMA) can exacerbate these adverse health effects by further increasing an Ecstasy user's body temperature. Also, due to uncertainties about the purity of MDMA, it can be difficult to know the dose of the drug; bad trips and other adverse effects can result from taking too much MDMA.

TOLERANCE

As the body becomes tolerant to the effects of a drug, users need to take ever-increasing quantities of the substance to achieve the same effects experienced at lower doses. This is why tolerance is such an important characteristic of dependence on certain drugs.

Multiple studies have shown that tolerance to hallucinogens such as LSD, mescaline, psilocybin, and psilocin builds very quickly; after three to four days of drug taking, the user does not experience any psychedelic effect regardless of the dose of the drug. Researchers have also discovered that once tolerance to these hallucinogens has been achieved, the user only has to abstain from the drug for about four days to once again experience the full effect of the hallucinogen. Experts therefore agree that tolerance-driven dependency upon these drugs is virtually unknown since tolerance tends to limit the frequency of their use.

MDMA is rather unique in this group of hallucinogens with regard to tolerance, and, to some extent, dependency. Tolerance to the euphoric sensations from Ecstasy develops quickly in a fashion similar to other hallucinogens. As a result, users sometimes take escalating doses of the drug to prolong their pleasant effects (called "stacking"). However, as tolerance builds, increased use of MDMA results in an escalation of the more stimulating aspects of the drug (described as "unpleasant") along with a decrease in the euphoria and openness associated with Ecstasy. Users also report combining alcohol, marijuana, or other drugs with these stacked doses of MDMA. Researchers and physicians cite evidence that many of these accelerated efforts to sustain a good trip with MDMA can pose unpredictable physical and psychological dangers to the user, and more often than not result in a bad trip.

Interestingly, when users are tolerant to LSD, they also become tolerant to mescaline and psilocybin as well. This is called *cross-tolerance*—one becomes tolerant to the effects of all hallucinogens simply by taking one frequently. It is unclear whether MDMA is cross-tolerant with any other hallucinogens. Its structural and chemical similarity to mescaline leads some researchers to conclude that MDMA may very well be cross-tolerant with these other hallucinogens. However, other researchers disagree and base their hypothesis on evidence that there is no cross-tolerance between LSD (and other related hallucinogens) and non-hallucinogenic amphetamines. Since MDMA is an amphetamine derivative, these researchers conclude that MDMA cannot be cross-tolerant with the other hallucinogens.

4

The Health Effects of Hallucinogens

THE EFFECTS OF HALLUCINOGENS ON THE CENTRAL NERVOUS SYSTEM

Drugs do not contain highs; they trigger highs. The potential for feeling high exists naturally within the human nervous system and we have countless options for getting high without taking drugs. Small children love to spin wildly in circles—so do Sufi dancers (a.k.a. "Whirling Dervishes") for that matter! Many people go sky diving, fall in love, paint, or meditate; the list is endless.

Hallucinogens trigger a high via the central nervous system (CNS). The CNS controls the functions of the brain and the spinal cord. There are billions of nerve cells (neurons) within the CNS that are linked by an intricate web of synapses (the gaps between neurons). Perhaps you seek to move a finger to relieve the itch of a bug bite. To do this, the neurons responsible for moving your finger need to communicate with each other. The message "move my finger" is transmitted simultaneously along the neuronal system of synapses via neurotransmitters. These neurotransmitters, or chemical messengers, are released by the neurons to help neurons communicate with each other.

Neurotransmitters can be visualized as keys that unlock specific sites on neurons called receptors. A neurotransmitter opens the receptor's lock, and it is through this "key" and "lock" system that messages are conveyed throughout the CNS. Most receptors are specifically tuned to accept only one type of neurotransmitter key.

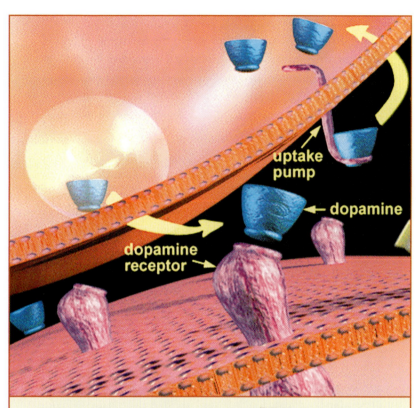

uptake
pump

dopamine

dopamine
receptor

Neurons in the central nervous system are linked by an intricate web of synapses. Neurotransmitters, like dopamine in this diagram, are chemicals released by one neuron and received by another neuron at a site called a receptor. The neurotransmitter can be visualized as a "key" that opens a receptor's "lock." It is through this system that messages are passed throughout the central nervous system.

Some neurons have thousands of receptors that are specific to particular neurotransmitters. The primary job of the neurotransmitter is to fit or "lock" into its own particular receptor and then to initiate specific physiological responses within the body. Once the message has been delivered by the neurotransmitter to the neuron, the neurotransmitter is either destroyed or reabsorbed into the neuron that released it. This whole process is called neurotransmission.

AGONISTS AND ANTAGONISTS

Many drugs are able to bind or attach themselves to a specific receptor, thus mimicking or blocking the normal function of the neurotransmitter destined for that receptor. Some drugs are agonists that activate or "turn on" receptors, while other drugs are antagonists that block or inhibit receptor function; both prevent normal physiological processes from occurring. The agonist/antagonist relationship is even more complex; many receptors in the brain are linked so that activation of one may block the function of another. These linkages are created by a variety of cellular messengers whose function is to relay information from inside neurons or from one neuron to another. Thus, proper functioning of the nervous system relies on balancing the results of these receptor activations. This is true whether the receptor is activated by a drug mimicking a neurotransmitter, blocking a neurotransmitter, or by the specific neurotransmitter itself.

THE AUTONOMIC AND
SYMPATHETIC NERVOUS SYSTEMS

Hallucinogens interfere with or disrupt the actions of the autonomic and sympathetic nervous systems. The autonomic nervous system performs the most basic human functions automatically and involuntarily, without conscious intervention. One does not tell the heart to beat, blood to pump, lungs to breathe, pupils to dilate, or muscles to contract. These autonomic functions originate in the central nervous system.

Although the autonomic nervous system is connected to our higher brain centers—the areas where thought processing, problem solving, language, and emotions, among other processes, are initiated—it does not rely on these brain functions to operate. Nevertheless, because of its connection to the higher brain, the autonomic nervous system *is* influenced by our emotions. Emotions activate the sympathetic nervous system, a branch of the autonomic nervous system that responds to short-term stresses by increasing blood flow, heart rate, metabolic rate, and body temperature. For example, anger can increase heart rate. The sympathetic nervous system is also known as the seat of the "fight or flight" response.

HOW DO HALLUCINOGENS WORK?

Hallucinogens create their psychedelic effects by changing or modifying how the neurotransmitters—serotonin, dopamine, and norepinephrine—interact in the central nervous system. Scientists have discovered that hallucinogens actually have chemical structures that are very similar to those of the neurotransmitters; it may be that these structural similarities allow the body to be tricked into substituting the hallucinogen for the neurotransmitter. LSD, psilocybin, and psilocin are structurally related to serotonin. Mescaline and MDMA, in the amphetamine-related hallucinogen group, are chemically similar to dopamine and norepinephrine and, to a lesser degree, to serotonin.

It is important to realize that the hallucinogenic actions within the brain and body are not well understood. Although structurally related hallucinogens tend to share similar psychedelic effects, there are nonetheless subtle differences among them. Scientists are still searching for evidence that would explain why hallucinogens produce their particular psychedelic effects.

SEROTONIN, DOPAMINE, AND NOREPINEPHRINE: PSYCHEDELIC MESSENGERS

Serotonin is a neurotransmitter that regulates sleep, pain sensation, appetite, mood, sensory perception, aggression, memory, and body temperature; it often plays a role in helping us feel relaxed and at ease. The nerve cells that release serotonin are localized in a section of the brain called the raphé nuclei, which is located in the brain stem and lies just at the top of the spinal cord. The brain stem controls our autonomic processes, including, for example, breathing, heart rate, and blood pressure. Neurons in the raphé nuclei connect with the limbic system (the area of the brain that controls emotions) and many other areas of the brain.

Dopamine helps control the limbic system of the brain, creating euphoria and mood enhancements, and is also responsible for many of the body's activities, including motor coordination. This neurotransmitter is thought to be the primary chemical in the brain that promotes the experience of pleasure. Research has shown that hallucinations are induced by drugs that stimulate the release of dopamine into the body: drugs that block dopamine activity (such as anti-psychotics) reduce hallucinations.

Norepinephrine works through the sympathetic nervous system to increase heart rate and body temperature. Most norepinephrine receptors are found in a small section of the brain stem called the *locus coeruleus*, a part of the brain that integrates sensory messages from the eyes, ears, and other sense organs. (Serotonin receptors are also localized in this region of the brain.) Amazingly, this part of the brain has only a few thousand nerve cells but is connected to about a third of the entire brain! Because of this far-reaching ability, it is believed that norepinephrine is released in response to emotionally arousing events that provoke our five senses.

Psychedelics that stimulate the release of norepinephrine result in a "speeding up" (also known as "firing up") of neuronal activity in the locus coeruleus. This resulting burst of brain-cell activity could explain the phenomenon of eidetic imagery as streaming images accelerate inside the head or synesthesia as sensations get mixed up from hyperactive neuronal messages.

THE EFFECT OF LSD ON THE CNS

LSD primarily acts at serotonin receptors which are also called 5-HT receptors. However, research indicates that LSD may simultaneously act as an antagonist *and* an agonist at serotonin receptor sites. Let us briefly discuss how LSD both activates and blocks the release of this important neurotransmitter and also whether these interactions help explain LSD's hallucinogenic effects.

Serotonin receptors communicate with many regions of the central nervous system through a series of both inhibiting (antagonist) and activating (agonist) actions. Hence, the effects of serotonin are felt in numerous areas of the body. In addition, perhaps eight or more different types of serotonin receptors exist in the brain. This far-reaching influence of serotonin makes it difficult for scientists to pinpoint the origins of LSD's effect in the brain.

Serotonin is generally an inhibitory neurotransmitter. LSD acts like an antagonist; it inhibits, or blocks, the release of serotonin at the receptor, which may cause excitation of other regions of the brain. For example, LSD can deceive the nervous system by acting as a sort of serotonin "imposter" at receptor sites, which signals other parts of the brain that too much serotonin is present. Other cells get this message and slow their activity, which decreases the amount of serotonin in the CNS. This slowdown in serotonin activity actually causes hyperactivity (excitation) in the regions of the brain that help regulate our visual and emotional responses. It is theorized that the psychedelic visual and emotional effects of LSD may be a possible consequence to this hyperactive reaction.

While LSD inhibits the effect of serotonin in some parts of the brain, studies show that LSD is also a serotonin agonist that *increases* the amount of serotonin in other areas of the CNS. It appears that LSD specifically activates the 5-HT2 receptor (a subtype of the 5-HT receptor) to release serotonin. Some researchers hypothesize that this action on the 5-HT2 receptor may be responsible for LSD's hallmark psychedelic effects.

THE EFFECT OF MDMA (ECSTASY) ON THE CNS

MDMA increases levels of serotonin, dopamine, and norepinephrine in the brain. MDMA does not directly release

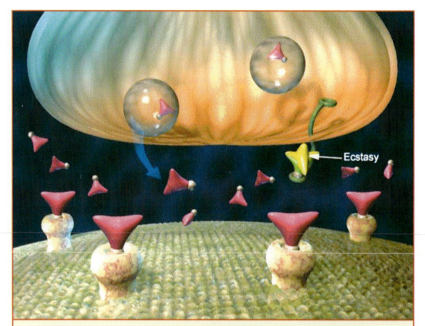

MDMA increases levels of serotonin in the brain by blocking the serotonin transporter involved in reuptake of the neurotransmitter. As more serotonin becomes available to the brain, it activates more serotonin receptors, thereby producing MDMA's psychological effects. MDMA acts similarly, although to a lesser extent, on the neurotransmitters dopamine and norepinephrine.

serotonin; rather, it binds to, and therefore blocks or inhibits, the serotonin transporter involved in its reuptake (reabsorption). (Transporters are the places on the surfaces of neurons that reabsorb the serotonin after it has completed its job.) As a result, more serotonin becomes available to the brain. This extra serotonin, in turn, activates an even greater number of serotonin receptors. It is this increased concentration of serotonin that is primarily responsible for the psychological effects of MDMA. In a similar, though somewhat less substantial way, MDMA also affects dopamine and norepinephrine, which in turn affect motor coordination, hallucinations, and stimulant-type responses.

It is important to note that many of MDMA's receptor actions are still unclear at this time.

CAN ECSTASY CAUSE BRAIN DAMAGE?

Some of the most recent and prestigious studies on MDMA and its effect on the brain provide evidence that chronic, long-term use of MDMA can cause serotonin neurotoxicity (brain cell death) in humans. Scientists funded by the National Institute of Drug Abuse (a division of the U.S. government) compared 14 MDMA users who had not used any psychoactive drug, including MDMA, for at least three weeks with 15 people who had never used MDMA. They discovered that the MDMA users had significantly fewer serotonin transporters in their brains. The dose of MDMA was directly related to these brain cell changes, with a higher dose correlating to greater neuronal loss. Researchers emphasize that damage to serotonin transporters in studies of MDMA in monkeys was still present seven years after drug use was discontinued.

These same researchers teamed up with the National Institute of Mental Health to ascertain MDMA's effects on memory, another serotonin-related function in the brain. This study compared 24 users to nonusers and found that heavy MDMA users had impaired memory that persisted for at least two weeks after the drug use was stopped. This memory impairment was also directly dose-related.

On the basis of these human and animal study results, scientists have preliminarily established that MDMA may be harming the neurons that release serotonin. Related studies show conflicting results as to whether the serotonin transporters regenerate after a certain period of abstension from the drug, whether other nerve fibers may compensate for the depleted serotonin cells, or whether serotonin levels in women are more negatively affected than in men.

Despite these areas of uncertainty, the evidence suggests that Ecstasy users may be permanently harming their brains.

For instance, some speculate that one possible long-term outcome of heavy MDMA use could be a type of serotonin imbalance, which is known to be an underlying cause of several mental illnesses, including depression, anxiety, and panic disorder. This concern is heightened by MDMA's extensive use among today's adolescents; many fear that thousands of teens will be at high risk for serious mental illnesses in the future as a result of their Ecstasy use today.

CAUSE AND EFFECT: A CRITICAL ANALYSIS OF THE EVIDENCE

Although findings of possible brain damage in adolescents are certainly alarming, many scientists, and even the researchers

DENTAL PROBLEMS IN ECSTASY USERS

The amphetamine-like effects of MDMA causes users to clench their jaws and grind their teeth for hours, resulting in serious dental problems. In a 1999 study conducted at a British facility specializing in drug-related medical problems, 60 percent of the Ecstasy users had worn their teeth through the enamel and into the underlying dentine. On average, the users reported taking Ecstasy about four times a month. (The dose was unknown.) Incorporating anecdotal evidence from users, the researchers hypothesize that the friction from clenching the teeth, along with an abrasive "dry mouth" (from the dehydrating effects of the drug), resulted in this extreme tooth wear. To preserve Ecstasy users' teeth, some dentists have prescribed orthodontic retainers for their patients. Many Ecstasy users suck on pacifiers to alleviate the sore jaws and teeth grinding that accompany its use. However, dentists caution that these pacifiers may add to an Ecstasy user's dental woes by exacerbating potential orthodontic problems.

who participated in the studies cited above, believe that there are methodological issues with most hallucinogen studies that confuse results. Therefore, before any hallucinogen, or in this case, MDMA, can be proven to be the direct cause of adverse health effects in humans, experts assert that more scientifically rigorous research must be conducted. (It is worth noting that these issues are also found in studies researching the *positive* health effects of hallucinogens.)

Overall, although the many studies conducted to date on MDMA's effects on the brain are cause for serious concern, the results remain preliminary and await the validation of further well-designed and comprehensive studies.

ADVERSE HEALTH EFFECTS OF HALLUCINOGENS

There is no generally accepted evidence that LSD produces chromosomal abnormalities or damage to a developing fetus. Studies have shown that there are no permanent changes to serotonin receptors even after massive doses of LSD are ingested. There are also no deaths attributable to the direct effects of LSD alone. A review of the literature finds few, if any, adverse health effects of psilocybin, psilocin, and mescaline as well. Some experts speculate that the lack of negative health effects of these hallucinogens may be related to the body's rapid development of tolerance to these substances, thereby limiting the body's overall exposure to these hallucinogens.

Anecdotal reports list suicides, accidents, homicides, and self-mutilations during or following the use of LSD and other hallucinogens. These reports lead some researchers to consider "behavior-related trauma" as one of the greatest adverse health effects of hallucinogens, rather than any specific toxic effects of the drugs. Others suggest that a bad trip is one of the biggest dangers of taking a hallucinogen. The most common psychological and physical adverse effects from a bad trip tend to originate from a user's acute anxiety or panic reaction during the trip; indeed, some users have required emergency room intervention or longer-term psychiatric assistance after using a hallucinogen. Panic and anxiety reactions to hallucinogens are successfully treated with support, reassurance, and a quiet environment. This approach "grounds" the user in the knowledge that the effects of the drug are illusions and do not represent reality. Most experts attribute bad trips more to the state of mind (set) and personality traits of the person taking the hallucinogen than to any chemical property of the hallucinogen itself.

Currently, there is no clearly defined set of psychiatric symptoms that can be directly attributed to hallucinogen use or abuse. Certainly, some hallucinogen users seek psychiatric services, but there are no data to indicate whether hallucinogen use is a precursor or consequence of psychiatric illness. There is some evidence that suggests that people with a history of mental illness in the family, or who have a diagnosed mental disorder, are at greater risk while using hallucinogens. This type of person has an increased chance of needing psychiatric assistance after hallucinogen use. Most experts agree that it is highly unlikely that the use of hallucinogens will cause a psychotic breakdown in those with emotionally stable personalities.

Current research indicates that heavy, chronic doses of MDMA may be neurotoxic, but the evidence is not yet conclusive. However, research indicates that low doses of Esctasy may be beneficial as a psychotherapeutic aid. Here again, we see the critical role of dose in determining the effects of hallucinogens. Experts await the results of additional studies to assist in more fully understanding these effects.

MDMA deaths, though rare, are possible. Heart attacks, lack of oxygen to the brain, and complications from hyperthermia (an excessive overheating of the body) have been linked to deaths due to MDMA. It is thought that stacking doses of Ecstasy, combining Ecstasy with alcohol or other drugs, or unknowingly ingesting MDMA that contains other, possibly more dangerous, drugs may also increase the possibility of adverse health effects.

Are teens more susceptible to adverse health effects if they use hallucinogens? So far, clear cause and effect data are inconclusive, but there are clearly potentially negative health consequences associated with the use of hallucinogens. What can be said with assurance is that studies have consistently shown that adolescents with psychological and behavioral problems are more likely than other adolescents to use drugs like hallucinogens. Therefore, while use of hallucinogens may add to a teen's problems, the roots of these problems may have existed prior to any drug use. Perhaps, in conclusion, it is the very unpredictability of these drugs that presents the greatest risk to human health.

5

Teenage Trends and Attitudes

OVERVIEW

Adolescent trends in drug use have been tracked for over 25 years. Researchers use this wealth of data to predict future drug trends and their possible implications for adolescent health and society at large. Patterns of drug use tend to be inversely related to perceived health risks. For example, in recent years, as knowledge of the health risks from cigarette smoking has increased, the number of teens who smoke has declined.

This inverse relationship, however, has not been evident in LSD and MDMA usage trends. In fact, LSD and MDMA have confounded predictions based on prior use trends. LSD use among teens has declined, but the number of teens who think they are at "great risk" of harming themselves by using LSD has *also* declined. Ecstasy use is on the rise among teens, but so are the perceived risks about taking it. As a result, MDMA use by teens is viewed as one of the most pressing societal issues of the twenty-first century.

Read on to discover more about these apparent contradictions in the adolescent use of LSD and MDMA, as well as other relevant trends in teen hallucinogen use. Special attention will be paid to LSD and MDMA since these are the two hallucinogens used most widely by adolescents.

HOW ARE TEENAGE TRENDS AND ATTITUDES MEASURED?

The U.S. Department of Health and Human Services (HHS) tracks the nation's substance abuse patterns through three major surveys:

The National Household Survey on Drug Abuse, the Monitoring the Future Survey, and the Drug Abuse Warning Network. Statistical information from these surveys helps the government identify potential drug abuse problem areas in order to set national drug policy and allocate financial resources that target areas of greatest need. Data from these large-scale surveys are also used to develop prevention and treatment campaigns, with particular emphasis on programs aimed at youths aged 12 to 17.

INTERPRETING THE DATA

A primary use of survey data is to ask questions from representative samples of the population, note patterns or trends in the responses, and then apply the discovered trends to the entire population. These three surveys address the broad category of

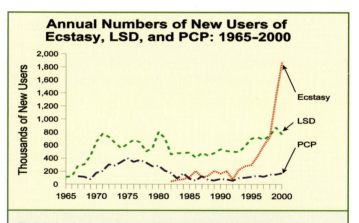

Annual Numbers of New Users of Ecstasy, LSD, and PCP: 1965–2000

Trends in drug use tend to follow a typical pattern: as the perceived health risks of using a drug increase, rates of using that drug decrease. However, LSD and MDMA use has defied this typical inverse relationship; LSD use has declined, but so has the perceived risk of taking it. MDMA use has increased along with the perceived risk of using it. This graph from the NHSDA tracks the annual numbers of new drug users from 1965–2000. Notice the spike in the number of new MDMA users in recent years.

"illicit drugs," which includes hallucinogens, marijuana, cocaine, heroin, inhalants, and several other substances. Marijuana use dominates this category; in fact, marijuana often accounts for 50 to 75 percent of all illicit drug use. Therefore, these reports often do not contain specific information about hallucinogen use.

However, knowledge about the broad category of illicit drug use provides us with a general background against which to compare specific teen trends and attitudes regarding hallucinogens. Since the use of illicit drugs knows no geographic or economic boundaries and is considered one of the most disturbing social problems in the United States, both general and specific information on this topic seems especially worthwhile.

An important role of the researcher is to interpret statistical information and understand its implications within a larger perspective. All statistics need to be assessed with a critical eye, because on the surface percentages and rates can sound so "official" that many accept their truth without analyzing the underlying assumptions that generated the statistics in the first place. For instance, it is important to note that the surveys cited here rely on self-reporting, a method that can contribute to under-reporting since teens may be reluctant to fully report their illegal drug use.

THE NATIONAL HOUSEHOLD SURVEY ON DRUG ABUSE

The National Household Survey on Drug Abuse (NHSDA) is directed by the Substance Abuse and Mental Health Services Administration. Since 1971, the NHSDA has provided annual estimates of the prevalence (patterns of use) of illicit drug, alcohol, and tobacco use in the United States and has monitored trends since that time. Results from this survey are based on representative samples of the United States population aged 12 and older. The illicit drug category includes marijuana, cocaine, heroin, hallucinogens, inhalants, and the nonmedical use of prescription drugs. Hallucinogens as a group include LSD, peyote, mescaline, mushrooms (psilocybin), and PCP, but only LSD and PCP are broken out of this subcategory in the 2000 survey. Little data is available on MDMA use; PCP use is beyond the scope of this book.

MONITORING THE FUTURE SURVEY

The Monitoring the Future (MTF) survey is funded by the National Institute on Drug Abuse. This survey has tracked illicit drug use trends and attitudes of eighth, tenth, and twelfth grade students since 1975. Students are asked about lifetime use, past-year use, past-month use, and daily use of drugs, alcohol, cigarettes, and smokeless tobacco. The illicit drug category contains virtually the same types of substances as the NHSDA. Hallucinogens as a group include LSD, MDMA, mescaline, peyote, psilocybin, PCP, and concentrated THC (the main psychoactive part of the marijuana plant). Data collection on MDMA drug use trends and attitudes did not begin until 1996; data collection on LSD and the other hallucinogens began in 1975. Although various data are available on each of the hallucinogens mentioned, LSD and MDMA drug use will be the focus of our report. PCP and THC trends and attitudes are beyond the scope of this book.

Despite differences in methodology, the NHSDA data and the MTF survey have shown similar long-term trends in the prevalence of substance abuse among youths. In addition to measuring prevalence, these surveys discuss teen perceptions of the harmfulness of drugs, their approval/disapproval of the use of drugs, and the availability of drugs.

THE DRUG ABUSE WARNING NETWORK

For almost 30 years, the Drug Abuse Warning Network (DAWN) has been an ongoing national data system that collects information on drug-related visits to a sample of U.S. hospital emergency departments (ED). The ED visit has to be directly related to the use of an illegal drug or to the non-medical use of a prescription drug in order to be recorded. These data are used to provide information on some of the

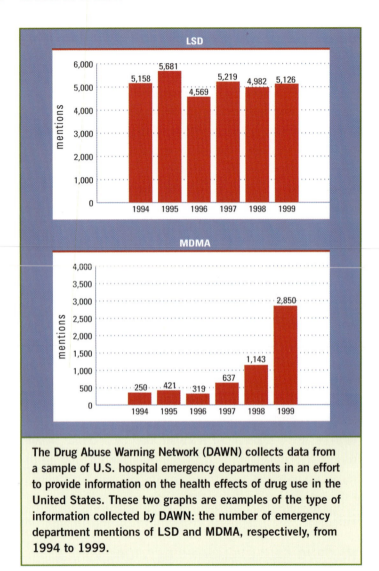

The Drug Abuse Warning Network (DAWN) collects data from a sample of U.S. hospital emergency departments in an effort to provide information on the health effects of drug use in the United States. These two graphs are examples of the type of information collected by DAWN: the number of emergency department mentions of LSD and MDMA, respectively, from 1994 to 1999.

health consequences of drug abuse in the United States. DAWN does not measure the prevalence of drug use in the population but does provide estimates of drug-related "episodes" and "mentions." An episode is the actual drug-related ED visit; the drug(s) thought to be responsible for the hospital visit are then "mentioned."

Since a drug-related visit to an ED can have multiple drug mentions (up to four different drugs can be recorded), not every reported substance may be, by itself, the cause of the medical emergency. DAWN researchers acknowledge this limitation of their data. DAWN, like NHSDA, is directed by the Substance Abuse and Mental Health Services Administration.

DEFINITIONS
Lifetime Use
Both the NHSDA and the MTF define a "lifetime user" as a teen who has used an illicit drug/hallucinogen at least once in his or her lifetime.

Current or Past-Month User
Both the NHSDA and the MTF define a "current user" as a teen who has used an illicit drug/hallucinogen at least once within the month prior to responding to the survey. This is also referred to as "past-month" drug use.

TRENDS IN HALLUCINOGEN USE
The 2000 NHSDA reports on current users of illicit drugs and hallucinogens as a group:

- In 2000, an estimated 6.3 percent of those aged 12 and older (about 14 million Americans) were current illicit drug users. Of that, 0.4 percent were current hallucinogen users (about one million) and, comparatively, 4.8 percent were current marijuana users (about 10.5 million).

- In 2000, 9.7 percent of adolescents aged 12 to 17 reported past-month use of illicit drugs. Slightly over seven percent specifically reported marijuana use. Thus, past-month marijuana use constituted an overwhelming majority (73 percent) of adolescent illicit drug use.

- In 2000, out of the approximately one million users of hallucinogens, 83 percent of them were between 12 and 25 years old, highlighting that hallucinogen use is more common among young adults than among older adults.

- In 2000, 42.7 percent of 12- to 17-year-olds who smoked cigarettes also used illicit drugs in the past month. By comparison, 4.6 percent of nonsmoking youths had used illicit drugs. In 2000, among 12- to 17-year-olds who were heavy drinkers, 65.5 percent were also current illicit drug users. Among nondrinkers, only 4.2 percent were current illicit drug users.

- Between 1967 and 1999, the estimated number of 12- to 17-year-olds using hallucinogens for the first time increased from 116,000 (1967) to 669,000 (1999). In 1999, nearly half of all first time hallucinogen users were 12- to 17-years-old.

- From 1965 to 1999, the age of first-time hallucinogens users has averaged 18.8 years, fluctuating by mere decimals from year to year.

Findings from the 2001 MTF survey tell us more specifically about LSD and MDMA trends among tenth and twelfth graders:

Lifetime use

- From 1997 to 2001, the number of teens who used *any* hallucinogen (with the exception of MDMA) at least once steadily decreased (from 15 to 12.8 percent for twelfth graders, and from 10.5 to 7.8 percent for tenth graders).

- In 2001, nearly the same percentage of twelfth graders tried LSD and MDMA at least once (11 percent used LSD and 12 percent used MDMA).

- Between 1997 and 2001, the number of twelfth graders who used MDMA at least once grew by 70 percent (from seven to 12 percent).

- In 2001, the percentage of twelfth graders who had used LSD at least once was similar to the percentage who used it in 1975 (10.9 versus 11.3 percent). This number trended steadily downward throughout the 1980s, and then began to rise significantly throughout the early 1990s. The prevalence of lifetime LSD use peaked in 1997, with the trend currently in a slow decline.

Past-year and past-month use

- Since the early 1990s, increasing numbers of high school seniors have tried psychedelic mushrooms. In 1992, 0.2 percent of high school seniors had tried mushrooms at least once in the past year; in 1997, that rate increased to about one percent. By 2001, it shot up to 4.9 percent.

- In 2001, 40 percent more twelfth graders chose Ecstasy over LSD at least once in the past year (9.2 percent tried MDMA; 6.6 percent tried LSD). More twelfth graders are currently experimenting with MDMA than with LSD.

- In 2001, 6.6 percent of twelfth graders tried LSD, but only 2.3 percent used it in the past month. With MDMA, 9.2 percent tried it in 2001, but only 2.8 percent used it in the past month. Few teens seem to use either MDMA or LSD in a frequent, monthly way, but rather seem to experiment on more of an occasional basis.

- Between 1997 to 2001, use of MDMA by twelfth graders within the past month increased 75 percent from 1.6 percent to 2.8 percent. However, past-year and past-month use of LSD among tenth and twelfth graders has shown a steady decline over the five-year period. Some experts hypothesize that Ecstasy is replacing LSD as the hallucinogenic "drug of choice," accounting for LSD's decline in popularity.

• Between 1997 and 2001, past-year use LSD decreased 40 percent in tenth graders (from 6.7 to 4.1 percent), and 21 percent in twelfth graders (from 8.4 to 6.6 percent).

• Between 1997 and 2001 MDMA increased 60 percent in tenth graders (from 3.9 to 6.2 percent). Most significantly, past-year use of MDMA in twelfth graders increased a whopping 130 percent (from four to 9.2 percent) over the five-year period.

It is important to note that the recent sharp increases in Ecstasy use are showing signs of slowing. Between 2000 and 2001, there was only a one percent increase in twelfth graders who used Ecstasy within the past year; past-month use of Ecstasy actually *decreased* by nearly one percent over that same time period. Survey analysts cautiously speculate that recent reports of Ecstasy's adverse health consequences may be contributing to this slight decline in its use. They look to next year's survey results to confirm that this is in fact a trend, not simply a minor statistical blip.

It is also important to understand that, while the *percentage* increase or decrease of use of either MDMA or LSD can seem quite large, the *actual number* of teens who use these drugs is extremely small compared to the number of teens who use marijuana. To illustrate this, it is useful to compare the number of twelfth graders who in 2001 either used marijuana, MDMA, or LSD in the past month: 22.4 percent used marijuana, 2.8 percent used MDMA, 2.3 percent used LSD.

Although much of the DAWN data does not correlate specific drug use with specific age groups, these data are quite helpful in providing an overall picture of trends in hallucinogen use. DAWN reports:

• In 2000, patients aged 18 to 25 and 26 to 34 had the highest rates of ED drug-related episodes, followed by patients aged 12 to 17. Patients aged 35 and over accounted for the lowest rate of episodes.

• From 1999–2000, total drug-related ED episodes increased 20 percent for 12- to 17-year-olds (from 52,685 to 63,443).

• In 1999, for *all* age groups, *all* drug-related ED episodes (554,932 in 1999) represented only 0.6 percent of the more than 91 million ED visits for any cause. Thus, drug-related episodes are relatively infrequent when compared to the number of ED visits for all other reasons.

• In 1999, LSD made up one percent of ED drug mentions; MDMA comprised only 0.3 percent. By comparison, nine percent of ED drug mentions were about marijuana, 17 percent about cocaine, and 19 percent "alcohol-in-combination." Additionally, over 70 percent of ED episodes involving club drugs also involve other drugs. Alcohol is the most frequent substance mentioned in combination with MDMA (47 percent), and marijuana is more frequently mentioned along with LSD (39 percent).

• In 1994, MDMA was mentioned very infrequently (253 times) in drug-related ED visits. However, from 1994–2000, MDMA mentions greatly increased (from 253 to 4,511 mentions, over 1,683 percent). In other words, MDMA was mentioned during one out of every 14 ED visits. However, this refers to *all* ages and is *not* specific to 12 to 17 year olds. It is also important to remember that multiple mentions are possible with each visit. Therefore, one cannot conclude from this information that MDMA was the sole cause of the ED episodes. However, large increases in ED mentions, as seen with MDMA, could indicate an emerging trend of adverse health consequences from this and related drugs; this trend will be watched closely over the next few years.

- In 2000, out of 63,443 total drug mentions for 12- to 17-year-olds, marijuana was mentioned 15,683 (or one out of four) times. MDMA was only mentioned 4,511 times by the entire population. This comparison helps provide context to understand these statistics more completely.

- DAWN data indicate that young people are disproportionately represented in ED visits involving club drugs. It is estimated that at least 80 percent of LSD, MDMA, and other club drug-mentions involve patients under 25.

PREDICTIVE FACTORS: WHY DO SOME TEENS CHOOSE TO USE HALLUCINOGENS?

Many researchers point to five factors that tend to predict the likelihood of hallucinogen use by teenagers: awareness, accessibility, motivations to use, reassurance about safety, and a willingness to break social norms and violate the law.

Awareness

In the 1950s and early 60s, most young people did not know much about hallucinogens and other psychoactive drugs. This awareness exploded in the mid-to late 1960s along with the Vietnam war, the "hippie movement," and other social protest movements that included "counterculture" activities. Thousands of young people "tuned in and turned on." The Beatles (and other popular music groups) sang "I get high with a little help from my friends" and "Lucy in the Sky with Diamonds," a reference to LSD. The use of psychoactive drugs such as LSD, magic mushrooms, and mescaline became a youthful expression of disaffection with what was viewed as the strict conservatism of the 1950s, and, more generally, the expression of a quest for experimentation and freedom.

The media played an important role in creating awareness of drugs such as hallucinogens, although not always intentionally. From news reports and "antidrug" advertisements to

Awareness of hallucinogens is one of the five factors researchers consider when predicting hallucinogen use by teens. Counterculture figures of the 1950s and '60s—like Timothy Leary, a Harvard professor who encouraged students to "turn on, tune in, and drop out" with the help of LSD— raised the nation's awareness of hallucinogens.

dramatic story lines showing favorite actors using drugs (whether advocating their use or taking an antidrug stance), the media introduced drugs to a mass audience.

Researchers and policymakers believe it is important to continually maintain and pass on awareness of the potential dangers of hallucinogens from generation to generation. In this way, they feel teens can make informed choices about hallucinogen use. This view is grounded in the theory of "generational forgetting"—the notion that it cannot be assumed that one generation will know the effects of using hallucinogens just because the previous generation knew them. These researchers and policy makers attribute the "rediscovery" of older drugs like LSD and the appeal of more recent hallu-cinogens like MDMA to this generational forgetting concept. They cite the increasing use of MDMA, along with a general decrease in the perceived risk of trying LSD, as evidence that each generation must learn anew about the potential hazards of using these drugs.

Accessibility

A link between the availability of drugs and their use has often been supported by statistical trends. For example, in 1999, NHSDA findings showed that adolescents who reported that marijuana was "fairly or very easy" to obtain were more likely to use marijuana than those who thought it was difficult to obtain. Can this finding be extended to hallucinogens? Let us analyze survey findings to decide.

The availability of hallucinogens to teens has been tracked by both the NHSDA and the Monitoring the Future surveys. In 2001, MTF asked, "How difficult do you think it would be for you to get MDMA or LSD?" This survey found:

- In 2001, 61.5 percent of twelfth graders agreed MDMA was easily accessible. Five years prior, in 1997, only 38.8 percent had easy access to the drug.

- Since 1999, this increase in availability of MDMA has soared about ten percentage points each year, from 40 percent in 1999 to 51 percent in 2000 to 61.5 percent in 2001.

- Between 1997 and 2001, the number of twelfth graders who find LSD "easily" accessible has declined from 51 percent in 1997 to 45 percent in 2001. Researchers believe that the decreases in LSD availability may be a result of the increas-ing prevalence of MDMA; if teens and their friends are using MDMA, they would have less contact with LSD-using friends who would normally provide that drug.

- In 2001, 41.4 percent of tenth graders found MDMA to be very accessible (as compared to 61.5 percent of twelfth graders). Findings from tenth graders mirrored those of the twelfth graders, albeit at somewhat lower levels of accessibility.

Motivations to Use Hallucinogens

There are multiple reasons why teenagers enjoy "getting high." Survey data over the years indicate that a majority of teens use hallucinogens such as LSD or MDMA to feel good, experiment, have a good time with friends, explore the inner self, and relax or relieve tension. According to these data, much of the motivation is celebratory in nature ("it's fun"), and many teens use hallucinogens in a social setting with friends. Ecstasy is popularly used at raves. Others may use hallucinogens out of a sense of curiosity or adventure, the desire to "fit in" with a group of friends, or out of boredom. Taking LSD is typically a planned and managed event, since set and setting are so integral to having a good versus a bad trip. For every generation, defiance of parents can be a motivation to use drugs such as hallucinogens.

Some teens use hallucinogens on a regular basis to deal with depression, anger, anxiety, or family/school problems. A teen who attempts to escape from his or her problems by getting high may have underlying psychological issues. This is especially true for adolescents who may substitute drugs as a coping mechanism in lieu of developing skills critical to living a full and functional adult life.

Reassurance about the Safety of Hallucinogens

Experts speak of "perceived risk" versus "perceived benefit" when attempting to understand teenage trends in drug use. Most of our everyday decisions are based on a balance-scale of these two ideas. When deciding to do something, all of us weigh the pros and cons—the benefits and the risks—and oberto, Katie, and Emily had decided to get some LSD about a month ago. It was all planned—parents were away for the weekend, tripping with their best friends, a fun escape from the everyday. Everyone except Katie had dropped acid before, and though she was excited to try it, she also felt unsure of what to expect.

"It's totally fun and cool," said Roberto reassuringly. "You'll see some weird stuff, like your senses are blending and melting together."

Emily chimed in, "I was in the back yard last time, sitting on the grass, and saw this ant. The ant turned into 50 ants a second later, but it wasn't scary or gross because then they all had instruments and became this ant marching band. I heard the tuba blow and everything!"

Roberto continued, "Just remember, it's all an illusion, Katie, everything you experience."

Katie asked, "Didn't Jake go bonkers on this stuff? He ended up in Saint Vincent's for a week, I think."

Roberto moved to Katie's other side, and shrugged. "He freaked. Dunno why, just that some kids do. I think it's because acid intensifies stuff, like whatever's going on inside your head," Roberto said, as he stroked her black hair, "from my experience, the more relaxed and happy you are, the better your trip is gonna be. Ya still in for it?"

Katie smiled, closed her eyes, and said, "I don't know. . . ."

Katie has a lot of questions about LSD. What her friends did not tell her, and may not know, is that every hallucinogenic experience is unpredictable. It is not possible to know for sure whether taking LSD, or any other hallucinogen for that matter, will end up being a positive or negative experience. LSD may not be addictive, but the issues of drug dependency are not that simple. Also, because the senses are distorted and altered, accidents and anxiety attacks are some of the most frequent adverse health effects of hallucinogens. Of course, hallucinogens such as LSD are illegal.

then make our decision. It is commonly believed that this risk/ benefit assessment is a primary factor in determining whether or not a teen will use drugs such as hallucinogens.

Additionally, studies show that information about the perceived benefits of a drug usually spreads much faster along teen grapevines than does information about the potential risks of that drug. It usually takes longer for evidence of a drug's risks to accumulate and then be disseminated. Thus, misinformation about the risks and benefits of using LSD or MDMA may be a significant contributor to their use.

It follows that when the perceived risks of using a drug catch up with its perceived benefits, the use of that drug will decline. This direct cause-and-effect link has typically been supported by survey results. For instance, an analysis of NHSDA surveys from 1979–1996 showed that 12- to 17-year-olds who perceived slight or no risk in occasional marijuana use were 12 times more likely to have used marijuana in the last year than teens who perceived great risk in using marijuana occasionally.

Interestingly, however, this has not been the case with LSD. Despite declining use amongst adolescents, there has also been a *declining* number of teens who think they are at "great risk" of harming themselves by using LSD. The 2001 MTF survey asked, "How much do you think people risk harming themselves (physically or in other ways) if they try LSD or MDMA once or twice, take LSD regularly, or take MDMA occasionally?" The findings from the MTF report indicate:

- Between 2000 and 2001, the percentage of tenth graders who thought there was a "great risk" of harming themselves from regularly using LSD dropped from 72 to 69 percent. In 2001, only 41 percent of tenth graders thought there was a risk from trying LSD once or twice.

- Between 2000 and 2001, there was a similar decline in perceived risk from regular use of LSD among twelfth graders (76 to 74 percent). However, fewer twelfth graders than tenth graders saw any harm in trying LSD once or twice—in 2001, only 33 percent thought so. Put another way, almost 70 percent of twelfth graders surveyed agreed there was little harm in trying LSD.

The trend that is occurring with teens who use MDMA also confounds researchers. The use of MDMA has been dramatically increasing over the past few years, yet the perceived risks have also been increasing, most notably since 2000. According to the MTF, between 2000 and 2001, the percentage of twelfth graders who saw great risk in trying Ecstasy once or twice jumped almost eight points (from 37.9 percent in 2000 to 45.7 percent in 2001). In 2001, about 40 percent of both tenth and twelfth graders perceived risks in trying MDMA once or twice. (The survey only began asking tenth graders about MDMA in 2001, so no comparative data is available from prior years.)

These trends defy previous logic and generate much speculation. What can explain: 1) a decline in adolescent LSD use with an accompanied decline in its perceived risks and 2) an increase in adolescent MDMA use with an accompanied increase in its perceived risks? The answers are not yet known but there is additional evidence to consider.

Further analysis of MTF data led researchers to conclude that there is an increasing number of schools in the MTF national sample who have at least one survey respondent who admitted to using Ecstasy at least once. Taking this information into consideration, researchers point out that despite increased perceptions of risk, MDMA is still spreading to new and different communities. This increase in the number of new Ecstasy users in more and more schools may be enough to offset the effects of the increase in perceived risk and seems to correspond with the steep rise in MDMA availability.

This may explain the MDMA portion of the puzzle, but we still need to examine current LSD trends. Researchers at MTF hypothesize that the reason LSD use is declining despite a decrease in its perceived harm is that another drug is displacing LSD as the hallucinogenic "drug of choice." MDMA seems the most likely replacement at this time, since it is the only hallucinogen on the rise at present and is generally used in circumstances similar to LSD. Future surveys may provide additional insight on these puzzling "countertrends."

Willingness to Break Social Norms and Violate the Law

Many experts observe that social norms about a drug are deeply influenced both by the drug's legal status and whether or not it is considered dangerous. Since hallucinogens are illegal and considered by many to be harmful, their use is discouraged by most of today's American society. Yet, teenagers as a group often rebel against societal norms. Hence, it is not surprising that many teens use hallucinogens or at least experiment with them, despite the consequences of clashing with parents, school authorities, and the law.

OTHER FACTORS THAT INFLUENCE THE DECISION TO USE HALLUCINOGENS

Teenagers cite numerous motivations for their use of hallucinogens, and researchers have generated an equal number of hypotheses to explain what may lie behind these motivations. In attempting to better understand the teenage thought and decision-making processes regarding drug use, much discussion has focused on several important predictive factors: personality type, peer influence and disapproval, and parental influence.

Personality Type

A teen's basic personality structure is closely woven into all other predictive factors of drug use. Researchers have long held the hypothesis that drugs cause a teen to behave or act in certain ways. Often, drug use in adolescence is associated with traits such as poor school performance, delinquency, acts of violence, laziness, and even mental health problems.

However, longitudinal studies on adolescents—studies that track the attitudes and behavior of the same "cohort" (group) of students over a period of time—support a very different hypothesis. Results from these studies have shown that teens who use drugs such as hallucinogens on a regular basis tend to already have fundamental psychological and behavioral problems. For example, recent research shows that regular users of hallucinogens, when compared with their peers, performed poorly in high school *before* they started using these drugs. Overall, although regular use of LSD or Ecstasy may add to a teen's problems, this latter viewpoint suggests that hallucinogen use may be more of a symptom than a cause of psychological and behavior problems. Indeed, it is suggested that if hallucinogens were not available, a teen with these types of problems might simply find something else to take its place.

Peer Influence and Disapproval

Peer influence appears to be one of the strongest factors affecting a teen's decision to use hallucinogens and other drugs. In fact, many researchers describe the influence of friends as "formidable" when referring to drug-taking decision-making processes. Various studies and surveys consistently show that if teens have friends who use drugs, they are more likely to use drugs themselves. Those who do not have friends who use drugs are less likely to use them. Many studies of teenagers report that there is no "forcible" peer pressure involved in the decision to take drugs.

Research also finds that teens taking hallucinogens tend to move toward new circles of friends who also use drugs, simultaneously increasing peer acceptance, access to these types of drugs, and the influence of other hallucinogen-using friends. Researchers emphasize that teenagers, particularly older ones, tend to associate with one another on the basis of similarities in lifestyle, values, and behavior. Drug use or nonuse has been determined to be one of those similarities, further enforcing the bond between friends who use or do not use drugs. In this way, teens often "self-select" and choose their friends based upon whether or not they use drugs; this selection process may be the "single most powerful factor" related to drug use among adolescents.

Parental Influence

In a recent magazine advertisement by the Partnership for a Drug-Free America (sponsored by the Office of National Drug Control Policy), a teenage girl is pictured with the text, "Sure, I want my freedom, but without parental supervision, I'm much more likely to smoke pot and stuff. I hope my parents don't try to act like my friends. What I really need is parents." The text along the bottom of the ad reads, "Talk. Know. Ask. Parents. The Anti-Drug."

This advertisement is based on research that shows that parents can influence a teen's decision-making process regarding drug use. Some researchers have argued that many parents fail to create or enforce guidelines or family boundaries surrounding the issue of drug use. Thus, this advertisement (one of many in the national campaign against drug use and abuse) is aimed more at parents than adolescents and invites parents to supervise and guide their teen rather than avoid the subject of drug use. In this way, the national ad campaign stresses the important role of parents in helping to deter their teenagers from using drugs like hallucinogens.

6
Hallucinogen Dependency

WHAT IS DRUG ADDICTION?

Drug addiction is a compulsive craving for a drug and has several components. One of the most important is tolerance—the need to use more and more of a drug to achieve the same effects. Since the body becomes tolerant to the effects of many drugs, users eventually feel less of an effect and therefore need to increase the dose of the drug to achieve the same high. This phenomenon of tolerance can increase a person's dependence on drugs.

Withdrawal symptoms are also an important component of addiction. When use of a drug is stopped, the user can experience a wide range of physical and/or psychological symptoms that will disappear if the drug use is resumed.

Drug addiction is apparent when use is maintained despite significant physical and/or psychological cost to the user or to the user's family and friends. Some experts expand the idea of addiction to include abuse, which they define as the use of any drug, illegal or legal, in circumstances that threaten a person's health or impair his or her social functioning and productivity. For example, a chronic user of LSD or Ecstasy can sometimes lose touch with his or her environment and peers. Missed school time and a lack of attention to personal hygiene and health can be signs of a teen who is abusing hallucinogens or other drugs—just as cigarette smokers who have chronic bronchitis, yet continue to smoke, are abusing tobacco. Thus, addiction, and by extension drug abuse, can be

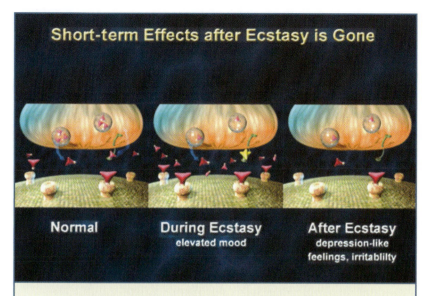

Short-term Effects after Ecstasy is Gone

Normal

During Ecstasy
elevated mood

After Ecstasy
depression-like
feelings, irritablilty

The short-term withdrawal symptoms an Ecstasy user may experience are caused by a chemical change at the neuronal level, as depicted in this diagram. Ecstasy use increases the concentration of the neurotransmitter serotonin normally found in the synaptic space (left), leading to sustained activation of serotonin receptors and an elevated mood (center). Eventually, neurons cannot produce serotonin quickly enough to replace that which was lost during Ecstasy use (right). Less serotonin is released with each electrical impulse, leading to feelings of depression and anxiety.

summarized as a compelling desire to use a drug, a need for ever-increasing quantities of that drug, withdrawal symptoms if a drug is not used regularly, and continuation of drug use regardless of circumstances or consequences.

PHYSICAL AND PSYCHOLOGICAL
DEPENDENCE ON HALLUCINOGENS

Since all drugs have particular, self-defining characteristics, experts generally speak of a drug in terms of the user's dependence on it, rather than the user's addiction to it. Though the two terms are very close in meaning, drug addiction is a special kind of dependence marked by physical changes in the body as a result of tolerance to and withdrawal from a drug.

Research shows little evidence of physical dependency upon hallucinogens. As with almost all drugs, hallucinogens can create some temporary, short-lived psychological dependency in the user. This psychological dependence can have many of the same characteristics as physical dependence—cravings, tolerance, withdrawal, and the continuation of the drug despite negative consequences.

We can sense, intuitively and practically, how almost anything can create dependency. Some teens say they "cannot live" without chocolate. Others may simply love to jog every day, rain or shine. Still others might read *Rolling Stone* magazine every month without fail or play poker for money every afternoon with their buddies. Researchers and teenagers alike often wonder, "How does psychological dependence differ from doing something repeatedly just because you like to do it?" Ongoing debate over the roots of addiction and dependency seeks to answer these types of questions.

Many researchers suggest that the essence of dependence lies in the limiting of personal freedom. We are all dependent upon food, water, and other people to live—no one is completely self-sufficient. However, what distinguishes drug dependency from other "needs" is that it can take over and control a person's life, often at the expense of virtually everything else. Some LSD users, for example, report that the illusory effects from the drug can "fool" them into perceiving "real" life as the illusion. This can delude users into thinking that their drug-induced lifestyle is representative of "normal" life and thus is essential for daily living. As each day or week becomes governed by how, when, and where drug use will occur, it is easy to see how drug dependency can limit personal freedom.

It requires a great deal of effort to break free from dependency on anything. Studies show that once a person becomes dependent upon a drug, there is often no route to ending the dependency other than abstaining from drug use altogether. Unfortunately, many people who try to end drug dependency often wind up switching one dependency for another. Hence, we can see that dependency on drugs, including hallucinogens, can be a very serious problem with many negative consequences. It is therefore important that we examine in greater detail the physical and psychological aspects of dependence upon hallucinogens.

PHYSICAL DEPENDENCE

Some hallucinogen users do develop a set of short-lived physical withdrawal symptoms. For example, chronic, habitual LSD users sometimes experience temporary withdrawal symptoms such as restlessness or depression for a few days after stopping the drug. A few cases of dependence on MDMA have also been reported, with chronic users experiencing brief withdrawal symptoms similar to those from amphetamines— restlessness, sleep disturbances, and jitteriness.

Nevertheless, an overwhelming majority of researchers consider hallucinogens to be non-addicting and non-dependency forming. Studies show that most hallucinogen users do not experience withdrawal effects after stopping use of these drugs; many correlate the ease of withdrawal to the rapid tolerance that develop to hallucinogens. Indeed, according to the 2001 Monitoring the Future survey, few teens seem to use either MDMA or LSD in a frequent, monthly way, but rather seem to experiment on more of an occasional basis.

Looking specifically at MDMA, tolerance seems to limit frequent dosing of MDMA. As tolerance develops in the MDMA user, escalating doses decrease the drug's euphoric effects while increasing the stimulating amphetamine aspects of the drug. Many Ecstasy users find these latter effects uncomfortable and unpleasant, leading them the stop the drug. Current data suggests that infrequent, low-dose use of

MDMA does not create the same tolerance and withdrawal patterns as high-dose usage.

PSYCHOLOGICAL DEPENDENCE

In attempting to predict future drug use by looking at current patterns of use, studies have shown that it is possible to be psychologically dependent on a drug without being physically dependent on it. For instance, after spending time in jail or in a treatment facility, many drug users often go back to using drugs despite the fact that their physical cravings and/or withdrawal symptoms have long since passed. Research shows that physical dependence is "all or nothing"—the drug is either addicting or it is not—while psychological dependence operates on more of a continuum. Some drugs create more psychological dependence (cocaine is high on this continuum), while others do not (hallucinogens are low on this continuum). Most scientific research shows that psychological dependence on hallucinogens varies greatly from drug to drug but is usually neither intense nor long-lived.

TEENS AT RISK OF HALLUCINOGEN DEPENDENCY

Because individual motivations to use drugs can vary so greatly, it can be difficult to know which teens will experiment with hallucinogens and then stop, and which teens will use hallucinogens on a more regular basis. Although any adolescent can develop a drug dependency, some are at higher risk than others.

Despite these predictive challenges, teenagers at risk for developing an abusive relationship with hallucinogens can include those who:

- Live with family conflict and discord. Adolescents whose parents are often in conflict, frequently absent, or inconsistent in setting boundaries and guidance are more likely to use illegal drugs. Teens may use hallucinogens to cope with family stress, low self-esteem, depression, anger, and anxiety.

- Do not fit in with peers. Some adolescents, particularly those girls who physically mature sooner than others, may feel out of place. Cognitive differences—from attention deficit syndrome to extraordinary intelligence—can put some distance between students and their contemporaries. Those excluded from the mainstream may find that drug use means ready acceptance among a cluster of new friends.

- Associate with drug-using friends. As discussed earlier, peer influence is one of the strongest factors in predicting hallucinogen use among teens.

REINFORCEMENT: The Key Motivator

One of the keys to understanding psychological dependence on hallucinogens is the concept of "reinforcement," which is viewed by many experts as the underlying motivator of drug-taking behavior. Indeed, some researchers believe that psychological dependence, based on reinforcement, is the driving force behind drug addiction. Reinforcement occurs when a teen receives a pleasurable sensation from using hallucinogens and is then motivated to use hallucinogens again to achieve the same pleasurable experience. The intensity of the pleasure that a drug delivers to the user is also a reinforcer of the experience. According to studies, taking an intensely pleasurable drug over a period of time leads to a powerful desire to repeat the experience (perhaps at the expense of personal or scholastic conduct).

In a similar way, research has shown that negative or bad trip experiences are equally as reinforcing as good trip experiences. Many teens have reported that it only took one profoundly bad experience while under the influence of hallucinogens to permanently stop using the drug.

Achieving pleasant or euphoric moods is clearly a perceived benefit of hallucinogen use. It is equally important to recognize that avoiding unpleasant moods or situations

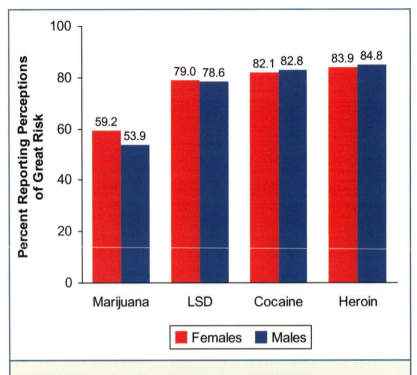

Drug use among teens continues even though more than 50 percent of the 70,000 males and females aged 12 and older polled for the 1999 National Household Survey on Drug Abuse felt that using marijuana, LSD, cocaine, or heroin placed them at great risk.

can be another important motivator which provides another dimension of reinforcement. Both experiences—pleasure or avoidance of pain or sadness—can lead the teen hallucinogen user to become psychologically dependent on hallucinogens. In fact, researchers believe that teens who use hallucinogens to seek relief from emotional pains such as anger, depression, or family/school problems are experiencing even stronger reinforcement for repeated hallucinogen use than those motivated by a desire for "euphoria."

Certain routes of exposure to a drug are more reinforcing than others. The quicker a drug enters the bloodstream, the faster it gets to the brain, and the sooner its euphoric effects will be experienced by the drug user. Thus, drugs that are injected or smoked have been found to be more physically (and psychologically) dependency-forming than drugs such as hallucinogens, which are most frequently eaten. The entry of ingested drugs into the bloodstream is slowed down by the digestive process, thereby delaying the time it takes to reach the brain. Injected and smoked drugs bypass this digestive process, and have more direct access to the brain.

PREVENTING HALLUCINOGEN USE:
What Works, What Doesn't

It is the opinion of many educators, researchers, policymakers, and social scientists that prevention of drug abuse is easier than, and preferable to, treatment for drug abuse. The earlier a possible drug dependency is identified in a drug user, the better the chance of correcting it. For example, researchers tell us that by understanding the predictive factors of teen hallucinogen use, young children can be identified as "at risk" for use of drugs prior to using drugs. They suggest that informing potential young users about the negative effects and risks of hallucinogen use (or any drug), as well as exploring drug alternatives, may be an effective prevention tool.

Current U.S. antidrug education and prevention campaigns increased in reach and frequency in the 1980s. Since then, adolescents have seen antidrug messages seemingly everywhere: on shopping bags, comic books, restaurant place mats, billboards, television, bumper stickers, and candy wrappers. Beginning in elementary school, the DARE (Drug Abuse Resistance Education) program sends uniformed police officers into schools to teach about the dangers of drugs. Researchers tell us that today's teenagers have had more drug education than any group of young people in American history.

In fact, it is estimated that over 80 percent of 12- to 17-year-olds have either seen or heard a drug prevention message outside of school in the past year; nearly the same percent have been exposed to a drug prevention message inside of school. Yet, as we saw in Chapter 5, past-year use of MDMA increased 130 percent among twelfth graders and 60 percent among tenth graders. Thus, antidrug education in America faces the challenge of a continuing trend toward increased MDMA (and other drug) use among teenagers.

ZERO TOLERANCE

The concept of "zero tolerance" drives much of today's legal and educational policy. The zero tolerance policies teach that using a drug such as a hallucinogen even once puts the user at risk for dependence and abuse of the drug. Most American drug education programs are built around this zero tolerance message. Proponents of this policy stress that the purpose of drug education is to prevent drug experimentation; therefore, the topic of drug use is practically forbidden. Additionally, as part of this zero tolerance policy, most schools impose

THE PROBLEM WITH ANTIDRUG ADS

There is little scientific evidence to support the effectiveness of anti-drug messages or their impact on the drug-use decisions of adolescents. Media campaigns such as the *Partnership for a Drug-Free America* have yet to be proven effective in the reduction of illegal drug use among adolescents. While these advertisements have been shown to strengthen antidrug attitudes among young children and non-drug using adults, similar effects have not been seen in the attitudes or drug-using behavior of teenagers. As an example, in a May 2002 news report, the head of U.S. Office of National Drug Control Policy, John Walters, announced that the antidrug advertising campaign aimed at American youth had failed to discourage teens from using marijuana and, in some cases, may have actually encouraged its use.

harsh sanctions, including expulsion from school, for any use or possession of drugs. As a result of this policy, many students are reluctant to discuss their own drug use in drug education classrooms.

Additionally, most school-based drug education classes fail to provide information on the relative risks of different drugs, doses, routes of exposure, or patterns of use. This presents a dilemma. Many educational and policy experts argue that the zero tolerance approach contradicts the natural propensity of teens to want to learn about, and possibly experiment with psychoactive drugs (a propensity that is evident in the recent trends in Ecstasy use and attitudes among teens). Thus, many experts observe that most drug education programs in American schools today do not provide much effective drug education.

In the 1970s, an alternative approach to drug education was endorsed by the National Institute on Drug Abuse. This approach, devised by researchers, psychologists, and drug-policy analysts, declared that the goal of drug education was to reduce drug *abuse*, not *use*. They argued that moralizing about drugs was ineffective, that exaggerating the dangers from drugs was counterproductive (and might even lead more youth to try drugs), and that expecting adolescents to be totally abstinent was unrealistic.

Although this prevention approach was incorporated into some educational materials for a short time, it was abandoned in the early 1980s during President Ronald Reagan's campaign of "Just Say No" to drugs. Since then, zero tolerance has been the predominant educational antidrug approach in American classrooms.

HARM REDUCTION

Based on the evidence that "Just Say No" does not seem to discourage teens from using drugs, many experts point out the success of "harm reduction" models of drug education. Proponents of harm reduction do not encourage or condone drug use, but they assume that many adolescents will eventually experiment with psychoactive drugs. Since their goal is to lessen the harms associated with drug use, these programs actively educate adolescents about the relative risks and responsible use of drugs. Most harm reduction education targets teenagers, since they are the age group most likely to experiment with drugs.

DanceSafe is one of several organizations that uses the harm reduction model to counteract the risks of Ecstasy use in club settings. This nonprofit national network group has volunteers in two dozen local chapters who promote guidelines for using Ecstasy as safely as possible. These volunteers work to reduce the risks associated with MDMA by interacting directly both with club owners and the drug users themselves. The "Safe Settings Campaign" urges club owners to "reduce the heat" in their establishments to lessen the major health hazard to teen MDMA users—dangerously increased body temperatures. These guidelines encourage club owners to offer free and accessible cold drinking water, provide adequate ventilation and/or air conditioning, have a separate "chill out" room for patrons, avoid overcrowding, and, for parties over 500 people, have licensed emergency personnel on site. In addition, Dance-Safe arranges on-site testing of the purity of Ecstasy tablets, since contaminants in MDMA are also linked to adverse effects.

Harm reduction is very controversial. Opponents believe it condones drug use and may lull teens into thinking drugs are safe. Proponents think it can save lives. In an interesting comparison of zero tolerance versus harm reduction policies, recent statistics show that 34 percent of those over age 15 in the United States (with a zero tolerance policy) have used the psychoactive drug marijuana at least once, as compared to only 19 percent of those in the Netherlands (which has a harm reduction policy). While it is possible that other factors affect these use patterns, there appears to be evidence that harm reduction does not lead to increased drug use.

Organizations like DanceSafe adopt a harm reduction model to lessen the risks involved with Ecstasy use. DanceSafe encourages club owners to reduce the temperature of clubs to combat the risk of overheating, one of the major health concerns for Ecstasy users. The organization also arranges on-site testing of the purity of Ecstasy tablets.

TREATING DEPENDENCE ON HALLUCINOGENS

Most experts agree that treatment for hallucinogen dependence begins with a user's own recognition that he or she is dependent on one or more of these drugs and that this dependency is a problem in his or her life. Many successful self-help groups such as Narcotics Anonymous operate from a philosophy that effective drug treatment is entirely dependent on an individual's motivation to change. Individuals who seek treatment assistance under duress or who are otherwise not motivated to take responsibility for their drug-taking choices are not likely to have successful treatment outcomes.

The majority of drug rehabilitation programs are designed to help manage the results of psychological dependence. These programs may include individual, group, and/or family counseling, often in conjunction with 12-step programs (such as Narcotics Anonymous). An overall goal of rehabilitation is to assist dependent drug users with identifying and understanding the motivators that drive their drug use. Most treatment programs incorporate group therapy; since many teens may not relate well to adults, some experts believe that effective drug treatment programs for teens need to be geared exclusively to their age group. They suggest that being with other adolescents who share the same problem is likely to be therapeutic for those who may feel isolated from their peers.

RECOVERY

Once a frequent hallucinogen user clears the drug(s) from his or her body and passes through any withdrawal symptoms, the journey to recovery begins. This is not an easy journey. It requires a complete reorganization and restructuring of thought processes, attitudes, and lifestyle. A hallucinogen-dependent teen may have organized nearly all daily thoughts and routines around obtaining or using LSD or Ecstasy, for example. Recovery involves a conscious and deliberate effort to create new, more socially productive ways of spending time in order to begin to focus on things other than hallucinogenic drugs. New focus can be directed toward work, hobbies, family, religion, and friends. In essence, experts suggest that recovering teens must entirely change their social structure. One of the hardest things for a teen to do is to stop associating with drug-using friends. As we have seen, peer influence is one of the strongest predictive factors of teen hallucinogen use. Conversely, it is also the most effective deterrent to hallucinogen use. Simply put, teens who do not approve of drugs are less likely to use drugs by themselves or with their friends.

Treatment programs of varying intensity exist, but all programs have the same fundamental mission. A hallucinogen-dependent person must maintain complete abstinence while learning to cope with the emotional and behavioral motivators associated with drug abuse. While most of the feelings or motivations for using hallucinogens may still exist, a great challenge for the recovering teen is to explore alternative ways of dealing with and expressing those intense feelings.

In many ways, this process is similar to dealing with the loss of a loved one. Recovering teens may need to grieve for the loss of their past history as they move into a new, drug-free life. During such periods of bereavement, teens can experience feelings of depression and emptiness as families, friends, and familiar locations elicit memories of past drug use. Looking back, recovering teens can see how this bereavement period is a natural part of change and growth. It is considered by many to be a healthy sign of a teen maturing to adulthood.

7

Hallucinogens and the Law

Hallucinogens are illegal to use, possess, manufacture, and distribute, yet recreational use of these drugs continues to gain popularity among today's adolescents. The U.S. Drug Enforcement Administration (DEA) has estimated that 750,000 tablets of Ecstasy are used every weekend in New York and New Jersey alone. Recent reports estimate that over two million tablets of MDMA are smuggled into the United States each week. At every level—local, state, and federal—the U.S. government attempts to control and reduce teen drug use through a variety of legal policies and procedures. Despite these efforts and harsh legal consequences that include jail time and heavy monetary fines, teens continue to use hallucinogens.

CURRENT U.S. DRUG POLICY: SUPPLY AND DEMAND

Does the supply of hallucinogens drive demand for them, or does the demand for hallucinogens create willing suppliers eager to capture their share of the very profitable illegal drug market? There are different points of view on this question, but any answer has implications for drug-reduction strategies. Those who argue that teens would not use hallucinogens if they could not gain access to them emphasize measures to reduce the supply, and therefore the availability, of these drugs. Others argue that more effective regulation is achieved through educational and treatment programs that prevent the use of hallucinogens and reduce their demand.

These United States Customs security agents guard more than 1,000 pounds of Ecstasy, which was seized in a drug bust at the Los Angeles International Airport in July 2000. Current U.S. drug policy attempts to reduce both the supply and demand for drugs like Ecstasy by reducing drug trafficking and educating users and potential users about the adverse health effects of drug use.

Current U.S. drug policy attempts to reduce both sides of this supply and demand equation. The 2003 budget for the National Drug Control Strategy, as requested by President George W. Bush, expands budgets for programs that reduce demand for hallucinogens and other drugs. Demand-reduction programs for 2003 include new approaches to drug treatment and basic research on drug use. The largest portion of the budget for demand-reduction programs is earmarked for educational and preventative programming directed to children and adolescents.

Budgets have also been increased for supply-reduction programs such as law enforcement operations targeting U.S. sources of illegal drugs, enhanced patrols along trafficking routes to the United States, and expanded security forces along U.S. borders (mainly in the Southwest). The 2002 National Drug Control Strategy budget was $18.8 billion; the proposed budget for 2003 is $19.2 billion.

Enforcing drug trafficking laws in the United States is extremely challenging. According to the U.S. Customs Service, each year 60 million people enter the United States on more than 675,000 commercial and private flights. Another six million arrive by sea and 370 million by land. More than 90,000 merchant and passenger ships dock at U.S. ports carrying more than nine million shipping containers and 400 million tons of cargo. In addition, 116 million vehicles cross the U.S. borders from Canada and Mexico. In the midst of this enormous influx, traffickers conceal drug shipments that are later distributed throughout the United States. MDMA, for example, is frequently smuggled into the United States by couriers via commercial airlines as well as through the use of express package carriers.

HALLUCINOGENS:
Schedule I Controlled Substances

The mission of the Drug Enforcement Administration, a division of the federal government, is to enforce the drug laws of the United States. The DEA is a principal force in reducing the supply, and therefore the availability, of hallucinogens and other drugs. The DEA was established in 1973 under the U.S. Department of Justice and is responsible for enforcing the guidelines of the Controlled Substances Act of 1970. This act provides the legal foundation for today's national drug policy. It places "controlled substances"—drugs that are regulated under existing federal law—into one of five schedules. Scheduled drugs are categorized by their distinguishing chemical properties, including their potential for abuse and their medical usefulness; drugs within each schedule often produce similar effects. Schedule I sets aside the most dangerous drugs that have no recognized medical use, while Schedule V classifies the least dangerous drugs as a group. In legal terms, any use, possession, manufacture, or distribution of the substances controlled in Schedules I through V of the Controlled Substances Act is considered drug abuse and is subject to state and federal penalties.

Under the Controlled Substances Act, LSD, MDMA (Ecstasy), peyote, mescaline, psilocybin, and psilocin are categorized as Schedule I drugs (as are marijuana and heroin). Schedule I drugs are defined as: 1) drugs with a high potential for abuse, 2) drugs that have no currently accepted medical use in treatment in the United States, and 3) drugs that under medical supervision lack acceptable safety data.

HALLUCINOGENS:
Manufacturing and Trafficking

Underground laboratories that manufacture illicit drugs such as LSD and MDMA depend upon special equipment and the

POSSESSION AND THE LAW

The manufacture and distribution of drugs usually carries stricter penalties than simple possession, but it is important to note that even the possession of a small, "recreational" amount of a hallucinogen can be considered "intent to distribute." From a legal perspective, money does not have to be exchanged for a drug transaction to have taken place. Merely giving a friend a dose of Ecstasy or LSD can be considered dealing and subject to harsh legal penalties.

availability of chemical precursors—non-hallucinogenic forms of chemicals that can be transformed into hallucinogens. To further reduce the supply of these drugs, the Controlled Substances Act was amended in the 1980s to classify these chemical precursors as Schedule I drugs as well, closing a loophole that had allowed illegal drug manufacturers to legally obtain the ingredients to make these hallucinogens. This led to the Chemical Diversion and Trafficking Act of 1988, under which 12 precursor chemicals, along with tableting and encapsulating machines, became strictly regulated by the DEA. Additional chemical control laws have been enacted since; currently 35 chemical precursors are regulated by the DEA.

Let us specifically discuss the illicit manufacturing and drug trafficking of MDMA, LSD, and magic mushrooms (psilocybin and psilocin).

MDMA

According to the DEA, about 80 percent of the manufacture of Ecstasy occurs in the Netherlands and Belgium. Organized crime centers in Israel and Russia, along with Western European drug traffickers, are the primary sources of MDMA drug trafficking. A small number of MDMA laboratories operate within the United States; in 2001, U.S. law enforcement agents seized 17 underground MDMA laboratories. In 1998, 750,000 MDMA pills were confiscated; just two years later, 9.3 million MDMA pills were seized.

Many MDMA traffickers use Montreal and Toronto as "transit points" on their way to the United States. In December 2000, the Royal Canadian Mounted Police seized approximately 150,000 MDMA tablets in Toronto that had been shipped by an Israeli MDMA trafficking organization from Belgium via DHL (an overnight mail delivery service). Many of the precursor chemicals needed to produce MDMA are available in Canada. The Royal Canadian Mounted Police estimate that the total potential yield of MDMA confiscated from illegal Canadian laboratories since 1999 is in excess of ten million tablets. Presently the United States and Canada are working together to curtail the legal availability of these MDMA precursor chemicals.

In September 2002, a DEA investigation called "Operation Spy Games" resulted in indictments of 34 members of one of the largest international Ecstasy trafficking groups in the world that included people from the United States, Spain, Canada, Israel, and the Netherlands.

MDMA is typically distributed at raves. The cost to produce it is about 50 cents per tablet. Prices for Ecstasy in the United States generally range from $20 to $30 per dose; prices as high as $40 per dose have been reported in New York City.

LSD

LSD has been illegally manufactured in the United States since the 1960s. Although the drug is primarily manufactured in Northern California, the Pacific Northwest, and, more recently, the Midwest, it is available throughout the entire country. LSD is typically manufactured using the chemicals lysergic acid, lysergic acid amide, or ergotamine tartrate. Lysergic acid and lysergic acid amide are both Schedule III substances, and ergotamine tartrate is regulated under the Domestic Chemical Diversion and Control Act. Difficulty in obtaining these regulated chemical precursors limits the number of clandestine laboratories manufacturing LSD. In 2000, the DEA seized an LSD laboratory that was located in a converted missile silo in Kansas.

Interestingly, LSD is widely available for sale via the Internet; thus, the buyers do not know the sellers, and neither do the drug law enforcement agencies. LSD is most likely to be distributed at rock concerts or raves. A "hit" of LSD can range from $1 to $12, but the average cost is $3 to $6 per dose.

Psilocybin and Psilocin

The hallucinogenic chemical components of psilocybin and psilocin are very costly to reproduce. This greatly limits any production of these drugs in synthetic forms such as pills or capsules. Prices for hallucinogenic mushrooms vary but usually cost about $20 for one-eighth of an ounce and $100 to $150 for an ounce. During a large governmental drug raid in 1999, federal, state, and local agencies—including the DEA and the FBI—seized 66 pounds of dried magic mushrooms and 100 pounds of fresh psychedelic mushrooms in Oregon. The supplier had been distributing these mushrooms to 11 states across the country.

DRUG LAWS AND PENALTIES

The legal history of drugs is varied, complicated, and continually changing. Although this makes a comprehensive summary of drug laws difficult, there are three underlying principles that help provide an understanding of current U.S. drug laws. First, the levels of punishment for a drug violation are based on the amount of the drug that one possesses or distributes. Second, the penalties for a second offense are harsher than the penalties for a first offense. Third, state drug laws differ from each other and from those established by the federal legal system. (Even though some states follow the penalty standards set by the federal government, they are not required to do so.)

Possession of small amounts of some drugs can be considered a misdemeanor, while possession of larger amounts of drugs are often considered felonies depending upon the most recent definitions of the drug laws and whether the offender is charged with a state or federal drug law violation. A misdemeanor is a civil offense that might result in a fine, public service, or a short prison sentence (less than one year). A felony is a criminal offense; once convicted, felons not only face massive fines and lengthy prison terms, but also lose the ability to obtain student and small-business loans, governmental grants and employment, and even rights of American citizenship as basic as voting.

The federal penalties for drug trafficking are harsh. A *first offense* conviction for the possession, manufacture, or distribution of one to nine grams of LSD (in mixture form) carries a five- to 40-year jail sentence along with a fine of up to two million dollars. A *second offense* conviction for the same amount of LSD carries a ten-year to life jail sentence and a fine of up to four million dollars. These penalties increase if even larger quantities of LSD are involved.

Federal and state sentencing guidelines are continually being modified. Until recently, a person convicted of selling 11,000 MDMA pills could receive up to a five-year jail term under federal law. As of 2001, the severity of this federal penalty increased; a convicted drug trafficker could receive the same five-year jail sentence for selling 800 pills. A New York State law, enacted in 1996, is tougher than the federal standard, requiring a minimum sentence of three years for possession of 100 MDMA pills. In 2001, Illinois created one of the toughest state drug laws in the country, earning a convicted drug dealer a mandatory four years in jail for selling as few as 15 MDMA pills. Even as this book goes to press, state and federal legal authorities are reshaping the laws and penalties governing hallucinogens.

HALLUCINOGENS AND THE JUVENILE JUSTICE SYSTEM

The first juvenile court in the United States was established in Illinois in 1899. The juvenile justice system was founded on the principle of rehabilitation, with a focus on the offender, not the offense. In the 1950s and 1960s, many experts began to question the ability of the juvenile court to effectively rehabilitate delinquent youth; by the 1980s, the pendulum began to swing away from this rehabilitative approach toward more severe sanctions for juvenile offenders. By the 1990s, this turn-about was completed as authorities more strongly enforced the legal standards of juvenile crime.

THE CONTROVERSIAL LEGAL HISTORY OF PSYCHEDELICS

The use of hallucinogens has always been controversial in modern U.S. legal history. Will researchers prove that hallucinogens have medical or psychiatric benefits for people with conditions such as post-traumatic stress syndrome, alcoholism, or obsessive-compulsive disorder? Are the members of the Native American Church being denied their right to religious freedom because they cannot use peyote legally as part of their spiritual rituals? These and similar questions abound. Let us briefly examine the histories of peyote, LSD, and MDMA from a legal perspective. Perhaps then you will be able to answer these questions for yourself!

PEYOTE AND THE NATIVE AMERICAN CHURCH

The worship of peyote by Native Americans as a sacramental spiritual symbol dates back 10,000 years. In modern history, the Native American Church was officially incorporated in 1918 to protect its members' religious freedom to use peyote in their ceremonies. Today, the Native American Church of North America has 80 chapters and members belonging to about 70 Native American Nations. With total membership estimated at 250,000, the Church is the largest religious organization of Native Americans.

The legal history surrounding the Native American Church has undergone many twists and turns. From 1965 to 1990, the traditional use of peyote by Native Americans for religious purposes was upheld by the federal government as a right protected by the First Amendment to the U.S. Constitution. (Peyote and mescaline remained illegal for anyone outside of the Church.)

James "Flaming Eagle" Mooney was charged with illegally distributing peyote to members of his branch of the Native American Church during religious ceremonies. Since 1990, the legality of peyote use in these ceremonies has been questioned. Currently only ten states uphold the Church's First Amendment right to use peyote under the Religious Freedom Restoration Act.

A mainstay throughout this time period was the American Indian Religious Freedom Act of 1978, which continued to uphold the Church members' religious rights. However, in 1990 the U.S. Supreme Court declared that a guarantee of religious freedom did not extend to the use of illegal drugs. This ruling was a result of a case that had been brought to the federal court by members of the Native American Church who were denied unemployment benefits after losing their jobs due to the use of peyote as part of their religious practice. Lawyers argued that members of the Church were being denied the right to practice their constitutionally protected religion; the Supreme Court ruled otherwise.

The 1993–1994 Religious Freedom Restoration Act restored the ability of the Native American Church members to practice their religion, including the ceremonial use of peyote, without fear of legal reprisals. However, in 1997, the U.S. Supreme Court declared the Religious Freedom Restoration Act unconstitutional as "applied to the states." Under this ruling, states were no longer required to uphold the First Amendment rights of Native Americans to legally use peyote in their religious ceremonies. Currently, ten states have the Religious Freedom Restoration Act on their books, and some members of Congress, as well as state legislators, are considering ways of fully restoring the constitutional protection of religious rights to the members of the Native American Church.

LSD: TURN ON, TUNE IN, DROP OUT

In 1947, after Sandoz's Dr. Hofmann discovered the psychedelic effects of LSD, the pharmaceutical company began distributing the drug to European researchers and scientists as an adjunct (addition) to psychotherapy. The company reported that LSD "would induce psychoses of short duration in normal subjects," which would facilitate the healing processes of the mentally ill patient.

In 1949, LSD was introduced to the United States at the Boston Psychopathic Hospital. By 1950, some of the first scientific papers were published supporting its use in psychotherapy. As more scientists and psychiatrists endorsed LSD's benefits, a symposium on psychedelic drugs was held at the annual meeting of the American Psychiatric Association in 1953. This symposium was addressed by author and novelist Aldous Huxley, an early proponent of the "carefully planned non-medical use of hallucinogens as a means to a higher consciousness." By 1960, researchers had presented more than 500 U.S. and international scientific papers on the therapeutic uses of LSD. In 1965, there were over 200 ongoing research studies using LSD and other hallucinogens on human subjects.

By 1962, LSD had become available on the black market; its hallucinogenic effects were to become one of the signatures of the youth and rebellion movements of the 1960s. In 1963, just as many researchers felt they were gaining a true understanding of LSD's enormous therapeutic potential, Sandoz's patent on LSD expired. Around this same time, the U.S. Food and Drug Administration (FDA), under the federal Food, Drug, and Cosmetics Act of 1938, moved to restrict LSD manufacture by classifying it as an "investigational new drug." This new status severely restricted the use of LSD in clinical studies; now, only researchers who received federal and state grants to use the drug could do so legally. Sandoz soon stopped production of LSD and turned over its entire stock to the National Institute of Mental Health. By 1965, researchers were required to turn over to the government any quantity of LSD left in their laboratories.

The first federal criminal sanctions against LSD were introduced in the Drug Abuse Control Amendments of 1965. Manufacture of hallucinogens (along with amphetamines and barbiturates) became a misdemeanor; possession carried no penalty. In 1968, these amendments were changed, and possession became a misdemeanor, while sale became a felony.

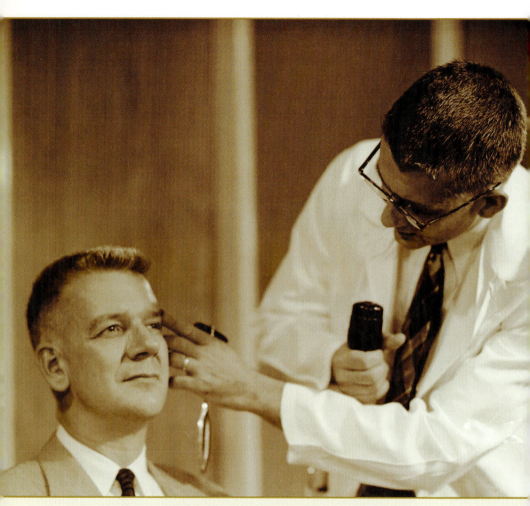

Some scientists and psychiatrists supported the use of LSD as an addition to traditional therapy, and studies using LSD on human subjects—like this study by Harry Williams (right) and Carl Pfeiffer in 1955—were conducted. LSD was classified as a "investigational new drug" around 1963, which limited its use in clinical studies.

Individual states were given the power to determine penalties, but most adopted the federal classification system.

As late as 1966, LSD was still being studied in about 70 research projects. Since access to the drug became even more restricted, only about a dozen of these studies remained active by 1969. The last National Institute of Mental Health studies using LSD in human subjects ended in 1974. In 1980, one private clinical study actively explored the role of LSD in alleviating pain, anxiety, and fear in terminally ill cancer patients, but was soon discontinued.

Today, the process of obtaining permission to study LSD on humans remains prohibitively complex. Nevertheless, animal research has continued, and the use of non-hallucinogenic forms of LSD has assisted researchers in evaluating the drug's effect on serotonin receptors. In 2001, researchers at Harvard University resumed the study of LSD's effects on fear and anxiety in dying patients with plans to conduct the study with more rigorous, scientifically sound standards than were used in earlier research.

MDMA AND PSYCHOTHERAPY:
Should It Be Legalized?

MDMA's ability to reduce defensiveness and anxiety without causing hallucinations is the underlying reason it was, and still is, seen as a potentially useful component of psychotherapy. From the 1970s to the mid-1980s, MDMA was used legally by a small but growing group of therapists. They were aware of the restrictions on using LSD in research, and so "quietly" went about conducting informal studies using MDMA. Roughly 500,000 doses were consumed in this time period with little publicity or notice taken by drug officials.

However, by the early 1980s, the word on the street was out. (This was similar to what had occurred with LSD in the 1960s.) Clandestine laboratories marketed MDMA as Ecstasy, and its recreational use exploded, alarming government officials and bringing media attention to the drug, which further enhanced its popularity.

In 1984, Senator Lloyd Bentsen of Texas formally requested that the DEA make Ecstasy illegal; later that year, the DEA announced plans to place MDMA in the Schedule I drug category. In the public debates that followed, the therapeutic community testified to MDMA's relative safety and unique therapeutic qualities, and requested a Schedule III classification (which would enable them to continue to legally prescribe the drug to their patients). Witnesses for the DEA stressed MDMA's abuse potential (due to its accelerated acceptance among adolescents) and its potential neurotoxic health effects.

In July 1985, MDMA became the first drug ever made illegal by the DEA's emergency scheduling authority (granted by the Comprehensive Crime Control Act of 1984). The DEA placed MDMA into Schedule I of the Controlled Substances Act for one year on an emergency basis. Ongoing debate continued, including the assessment of MDMA as a safe and medically useful drug.

In 1986, the DEA's administrative law judge recommended that MDMA be placed into Schedule III, concluding "there was sufficient evidence for MDMA's acceptable medical use and safe utilization under medical supervision." However, the DEA overruled its own law judge's decision, and in 1988 placed MDMA permanently into Schedule I.

This DEA scheduling effectively ended MDMA's therapeutic use and severely curtailed its role in controlled clinical studies. However, in 1995, an FDA-approved study revealed no unusual risks associated with MDMA use in a supervised medical setting, and in 2001, the federal government approved research on treating post-traumatic stress disorder with MDMA.

The current illegality of MDMA has not curtailed its recreational use by teenagers; as a result, lawmakers and other federal authorities have focused great attention on Ecstasy. Beginning around 2000, law enforcement policy regarding MDMA began to shift from an emphasis on users, manufacturers, and dealers of MDMA to the establishments and owners of venues where raves take place. Laws like the Ecstasy Prevention Act of 2001, the Clean-Up Methamphetamines Act of 2002, and the RAVE Act of 2002 (the Reducing Americans Vulnerability to Ecstasy Act) seek to reduce the supply of Ecstasy by shutting down the venues where it is primarily used.

A detailed examination of all these laws and acts is beyond the scope of this book. However, it is important to understand that many critics believe these laws will simply drive teens to use Ecstasy in new and different ways and places—venues that might be less likely to provide safety mechanisms that reduce the potential risks attributed to Ecstasy use. It is certain, however, that proponents of stricter drug enforcement will argue with equal conviction that the potential adverse health effects of MDMA and other hallucinogens demand a zero tolerance approach to these and other drugs.

Bibliography

Books

Goode, Erich. *Drugs in American Society.* 4th ed. New York: McGraw-Hill, Inc., 1993.

Grinspoon, Lester and James. B. Bakalar. *Psychedelic Drugs Reconsidered.* New York: Basic Books, Inc., 1979.

Henderson, Leigh A. and William J. Glass. *LSD: Still With Us After All These Years.* San Francisco: Jossey-Bass Publishers, 1994.

Huxley, Aldous. *The Doors of Perception.* New York: Harper and Row, 1954.

Jaffe, Jerome H. *Encyclopedia of Drugs and Alcohol, Vol. 1.* New York: Simon & Schuster Macmillan, 1995.

Jaffe, Jerome H. *Encyclopedia of Drugs and Alcohol, Vol. 2.* New York: Simon & Schuster Macmillan, 1995.

Lagassé, Paul (Editor). *The Columbia Encyclopedia.* 6th ed. New York: Columbia University Press, 2000.

Kuhn, Cynthia, Scott Swartzwelder, and Wilkie Wilson. *Buzzed.* New York: W.W. Norton and Company, 1998.

Ottomanelli, Gennaro. *Children and Addiction.* Westport, Conn.: Praeger Publishers, 1995.

Pellerin, Cheryl. *Trips: How Hallucinogens Work in Your Brain.* New York: Seven Stories Press, 1998.

Roza, Greg. *The Encyclopedia of Drugs and Alcohol.* New York: The Rosen Publishing Group, Inc., 2001.

Siegel, Ronald K. *Intoxication: Life in Pursuit of Artificial Paradise.* New York: E.P. Dutton, 1989.

Snyder, Solomon. *Drugs and the Brain.* Philadelphia: Chelsea House Publishers, 1987.

Weil, Andrew and Winifred Rosen. *From Chocolate to Morphine.* Boston: Houghton Mifflin Company, 1998.

Articles, Organizations, and Websites

Blakeslee, Sandra. "Scientists Test Hallucinogens for Mental Ills." *The New York Times.* March 13, 2001.

Butterfield, Fox. "Violence rises as club drug spreads out into the streets." *The New York Times.* June 24, 2001.

Cameron, Scott. "Hallucinogens." *eMedicine Journal (2002):* Vol. 3, No. 1.

Christian Science Committee on Publication. Obtained September 2002, from *http://www.religious-freedom.org.*

DanceSafe. Obtained September 2002, from *http://www.dancesafe.org.*

Drug Policy Alliance. *RAVE Act Analysis.* Obtained September 2002, from *http://www.drugpolicy.org.*

Drug Enforcement Administration. Obtained September 2002, from *http://www.usdoj.gov/dea.*

Dye, Christina. *Psilocybin: De-Mystifying the Magic Mushroom.* Do It Now Foundation, 1993, from *www.doitnow.org.*

Electronic Music Defense and Education Fund. Obtained September 2002, from *http://www.emdef.org.*

Johnston, L.D., P.M. O'Malley, and J.G. Bachman. *Monitoring the Future National Results on Adolescent Drug Use: Overview of Key Findings, 2001.* National Institute on Drug Abuse (NIH Publication No. 02-5105). 2002.

Johnston, L.D., P.M. O'Malley, and J.G. Bachman. *Demographic Subgroup Trends for Various Licit and Illicit Drugs, 1975–2001.* (Monitoring the Future Occasional Paper No. 57). National Institute on Drug Abuse. 2002.

Johnston, L.D., P.M. O'Malley, and J.G. Bachman. *Monitoring the Future National Results on Adolescent Drug Use: Volume 1, Appendix E.* National Institute on Drug Abuse. 2002.

Johnston, L.D. *Reasons for Use, Abstention, and Quitting Illicit Drug Use by American Adolescents.* (Monitoring the Future Occasional Paper No. 44.) National Institute on Drug Abuse. 1998.

Kalant, Harold. "The pharmacology and toxicology of 'ecstasy' (MDMA) and related drugs." *Canadian Medical Association Journal (2001):* Vol. 165, Issue 7.

Kandel, Denise, and Pamela Griesler, et al. *Parental Influences on Adolescent Marijuana Use and the Baby Boom Generation: Findings from the 1979–1996 NHSDA.* Substance Abuse and Mental Health Services Administration, Office of Applied Studies, 2001.

Mathias, Robert. "'Ecstasy' Damages the Brain and Impairs Memory in Humans." *NIDA NOTES* (1999): Vol. 14, No. 4.

Milosevic, A. and N. Agrawal, P. Redfearn, and L. Mair. "The occurrence of toothwear in users of Ecstasy." *Community Dentistry and Oral Epidemiology (1999):* Vol. 27, No. 4.

National Center on Addiction and Substance Abuse (CASA). *The National Survey of American Attitudes on Substance Abuse VI: Teens.* Obtained May 2002, from *http://www.casacolumbia.org.*

National Organization for the Reform of Marijuana Laws (NORML). *Unintended Consequences! Drug Czar Admits Federal Anti-Drug Ads Having Opposite Effect on Teens.* Obtained June 2002, from *http://www.norml.org.*

The New Encyclopaedia Britannica, Vol. 13, 15th ed. "Pychotropic Drugs." Chicago: Encyclopaedia Briannica, 2002.

Reneman, Liesbeth, Jan Booij, Kora de Bruin, Johannes B. Reitsma, et al. "Effects of dose, sex, and long-term abstention from use on toxic effects of MDMA (Esctasy) on brain serotonin neurons." *Lancet (2001):* Vol. 358, Issue 9296.

Rosenbaum, Marsha and Rick Doblin. "Why MDMA Should Not Have Been Made Illegal," in *The Drug Legalization Debate,* ed. James A. Inciardi. Obtained September, 2002, from *http://www.druglibrary.org.*

Snyder, Howard N. and Melissa Sickmund. *Juvenile Offenders and Victims: 1999 National Report.* Office of Juvenile Justice and Delinquency Prevention, 1999.

Substance Abuse and Mental Health Services Administration. *Summary of Findings from the 2000 National Household Survey on Drug Abuse.* NHSDA Series H-13, DHHS Publication No. (SMA) 01-3549. 2001.

Substance Abuse and Mental Health Services Administration. Office of Applied Studies. *Emergency Department Trends from the Drug Abuse Warning Network, Preliminary Estimates January–June 2001 with Revised Estimates 1994 to 2000.* DAWN Series D-20, DHHS Publication No. (SMA) 02-3634. 2002.

Substance Abuse and Mental Health Services Administration. Office of Applied Studies. Department of Health and Human Services. *The NHSDA Report: Availability of Illicit Drugs to Females Aged 12 to 17.* 2001.

Substance Abuse and Mental Health Services Administration. *Treatment Episode Data Set (TEDS): 1994–1999. National Admissions to Substance Abuse Treatment Services,* DASIS Series: S-14, DHHS Publication No. (SMA) 01-3550. 2001.

U.S. Department of Justice. Federal Bureau of Investigation. *Crime in the United States 2000: Uniform Crime Reports.* Washington, D.C.: Government Printing Office, 2000.

University of Iowa. Obtained August 2002, from *http://www.uiowa.edu/~shs/ecstasy.htm.*

Valentine, Gerald. "MDMA and Ecstasy." *Psychiatric Times (2002):* Vol. XIX, Issue 2.

The Vaults of Erowid. Obtained October 2002, from *http://www.erowid.org/freedom/religious/.*

Zimmer, L. and J.P. Morgan. *Marijuana Myths, Marijuana Facts: A Review of the Scientific Evidence.* New York: The Lindesmith Center, 1997.

Further Reading

Books

Alternatives to Drugs

Cousins, Norman. *Anatomy of an Illness*. Boston: G.K Hall, 1980.

Weil, M.D., Andrew. *The Marriage of the Sun and Moon: A Quest for Unity in Consciousness*. Boston: Houghton Mifflin, 1980.

Critical Thinking

Bakalar, James B. and Lester Grinspoon. *Drug Control in a Free Society*. New York: Cambridge University Press, 1984.

Goldberg, Raymond. *Taking Sides. Clashing Views on Controversial Issues in Drugs and Society (3rd Ed.)*. Guilford, Conn.: Dushkin/McGraw-Hill, 1998.

Dependency

Wilshire, Bruce. *Wild Hunger*. Lanham: Rowman & Littlefield Publishers, Inc., 1999.

Hallucinogens

Grob, Charles S., Ed. *Hallucinogens: A Reader*. New York: Jeremy P. Tarcher/Putnam, 2002.

LSD

Black, David. *ACID: A New Secret History of LSD*. London: Satin Publications, Ltd., 2001.

Grof, Stanislav. *LSD Psychotherapy*. Alameda, Cal.: Hunter House, Inc., 1994.

Stevens, Jay. *Storming Heaven: LSD and the American Dream*. New York: Atlantic Monthly Press, 1987.

Psilocybin/Psilocin

McKenna, Terrence. *Food of the Gods*. New York: Bantam, 1992.

MDMA

Holland, Julie. *Ecstasy: The Complete Guide. A Comprehensive Look at the Risks and Benefits of MDMA*. Rochester, Vt. : Park Street Press, 2001.

Mescaline

Huxley, Aldous. *The Doors of Perception* and *Heaven and Hell*. New York: Harper and Row, 1954.

Peyote

Stewart, Omer C. *Peyote Religion: A History*. Norman, Okla.: University of Oklahoma Press, 1987.

Websites

About.com Substance Abuse
http://substanceabuse.about.com

American Council for Drug Education (ACDE)
http://www.acde.org

Center for Substance Abuse Treatment (CSAT)
http://www.samhsa.gov/csat/csat.htm

DanceSafe
http:www.dancesafe.org

Drug Enforcement Agency (DEA)
http://www.usdoj.gov/dea/index.htm

Drug Policy Alliance
http://www.drugpolicy.org

Electronic Music Defense and Education Fund
http://www.emdef.org

FBI Uniform Crime Reports
http://www.fbi.gov/ucr/ucr.htm

Freevibe
http://www.freevibe.com

Hallucinogenic Drugs and Plants in Psychotherapy and Shamanism
http://www.rmetzner-greenearth.org/plants.html

Heffter Research Institute
http://www.heffter.org/

How Stuff Works
http://www.howstuffworks.com

Timothy Leary website
http://www.leary.com/mainline.html

Multidisciplinary Association for Psychedelic Studies (MAPS)
http://www.maps.org/

Monitoring the Future survey
http://www.monitoringthefuture.org

Narcotics Anonymous
http://www.narcoticsanonymous.com

National Center on Addiction and Substance Abuse (CASA)
http://www.casacolumbia.org

National Criminal Justice Referral Service (NCJRS)
http://www.ncjrs.org

National Household Survey on Drug Abuse (NHSDA)
http://www.samhsa.gov/oas/nhsda.htm

National Institute on Drug Abuse (NIDA)
http://www.nida.nih.gov

Office of Juvenile Justice and Delinquency Prevention (OJJDP)
http://ojjdp.ncjrs.org

Office of National Drug Control Policy
http://www.whitehousedrugpolicy.gov

Schaffer Library of Drug Policy
http://www.druglibrary.org

The Vaults of Erowid
http://www.erowid.org

Index

Picture Credits

About the Author

Randi Mehling holds a Bachelor's in Journalism and a Master of Public Health from Rutgers University. Throughout her career, she has combined her passion for writing with her interest in health care and the environment. In addition to writing nonfiction for young adults, Randi has published in academic journals such as *Trends in Health Care, Law & Ethics*, designed educational programs for chronically ill patients, is a published poet, and is currently working on her first novel. Her commitment to education has led her to teach martial arts to children and Spanish to adults. She and her husband, Rod, live in the New Jersey countryside.

About the Editor

David J. Triggle is a University Professor and a Distinguished Professor in the School of Pharmacy and Pharmaceutical Sciences at the State University of New York at Buffalo. He studied in the United Kingdom and earned his B.Sc. degree in Chemistry from the University of Southampton and a Ph.D. degree in Chemistry at the University of Hull. Following post-doctoral work at the University of Ottawa in Canada and the University of London in the United Kingdom, he assumed a position at the School of Pharmacy at Buffalo. He served as Chairman of the Department of Biochemical Pharmacology from 1971 to 1985 and as Dean of the School of Pharmacy from 1985 to 1995. From 1995 to 2001, he served as the Dean of the Graduate School and as the University Provost from 2000 to 2001. He is the author of several books dealing with the chemical pharmacology of the autonomic nervous system and drug-receptor interactions, roughly four hundred scientific publications, and has delivered over one thousand lectures worldwide on his research.